Simple guide to

creating and using spreadsheets

C. Penfold

Prentice Hall

iv

Pearson Education Limited

Head Office:
Edinburgh Gate
Harlow
Essex CM20 2JE
Tel: +44 (0)1279 623623
Fax: +44 (0)1279 431059

London Office:
128 Long Acre
London WC2E 9AN
Tel: +44 (0)20 7447 2000
Fax: +44 (0)20 7240 5771
website: www.it-minds.com

First published in Great Britain 2001
© Pearson Education Limited 2001

British Library Cataloguing in Publication Data
A CIP catalogue record for this book can be obtained from the British Library.

ISBN 0-130-60867-X

10 9 8 7 6 5 4 3 2 1

Typeset by Pantek Arts Ltd, Maidstone, Kent.
Printed and bound in Great Britain by Ashford Colour Press, Gosport, Hampshire.

The publishers' policy is to use paper manufactured from sustainable forests.

Contents

Introduction

No one who reads this book will be able to call themselves an expert spreadsheet user at the end of it. These days spreadsheet packages are just too big and feature-laden for any one book to even cover adequately, far less plumb the depths. To be an expert (or a pro or a power user) calls for a lot more than this book will ever supply.

The best anyone who reads this can hope to be is competent. Even so, competence is a vast improvement on most spreadsheet users, not to mention being the first step towards becoming an expert. As such, even those not interested in climbing to such rarefied heights will still find that a small investment now will pay huge dividends later.

Look at it this way. A spreadsheet is what is known as a productivity aid; it helps people work more productively. In other words it replaces long, laborious and error-prone human calculation with a fast, efficient, computerised method. All of which is very cost-effective, just so long as someone actually knows how to do it. Without that understanding, a cheap calculator would be a better investment, but with it a brand new world opens up, full of instant analysis, accurate data and a highly impressive grasp of management control information. In short, everything that turns just another worker drone into an indispensable asset – not bad for the price of a book and a few hours' work.

Needless to say that work will be at least as important as anything else this book might have to offer, if not more so. Nothing can replace the experience of actually using a spreadsheet. The only consolation is that they are nowhere near as difficult to use as they might at first appear. In their case a little learning can genuinely go a long way – providing that learning is backed up with practice, naturally.

Icons

These notes provide additional information about the subject concerned.

These notes indicate a variety of shortcuts: keyboard shortcuts, 'wizard' options, techniques reserved for experts, etc.

These notes warn you of the risks associated with a particular action and, where necessary, show you how to avoid any pitfalls.

Spreadsheet design

1

Before anyone can build a spreadsheet they have to know exactly what is required. That might seem obvious, but too often projects are started with only a vague idea as to why they should be done which, naturally, leads only to confusion – not to mention an abandoned spreadsheet.

The 'so that' question

The first lesson, then, is to have a clear understanding of just what is needed before starting to build a spreadsheet. According to the textbooks this is sometimes defined as conceptualisation, which is fairly self-explanatory, although a far better way of describing it is to say it is really all about asking the 'so that' question. For example, a spreadsheet to find the total number of products sold in a given time period might, on the face of it, seem like a reasonable request which needs no clarification. At least it does until the 'so that' question is asked. Then the problems become apparent because the answer might be, so that the best and worst sellers can be found; so that the sales per region can be compared; or so that sales per product per region can be analysed. These would all come under the heading of finding the total number of products sold and yet in every case a different spreadsheet would need to be constructed.

In fact it is the failure to have a clearly defined goal, or concept, which is the cause of most problems. If a spreadsheet is useful – and all spreadsheets should be useful – there will inevitably be calls for it to be extended, for it to do more. When that happens, if the expansion has not been planned for right from the start, it will be difficult to achieve and could involve more work than is justified. For that reason always be sure to find out exactly what is expected from a spreadsheet before starting to build it.

Even then more work has to be done before going anywhere near a spreadsheet. This is because a computer is too precise an instrument for vague notions as to how one piece of data relates to another. For a spreadsheet to work, both the relationship and the dependencies of each item of information must be precisely considered, and those relationships should be formally expressed. That might sound overly pedantic, but what it really means is that you should decide in advance what figures have to be manipulated to produce the desired results and exactly what form that manipulation should take.

For example:

REVENUE = PRODUCTS SOLD × SALES PRICE

That might seem like a straightforward calculation, too simple to be worth the bother of such an elaborate formal process, yet consider it further. Suppose some form of quantity discount was offered. If so, the formula for Sales Price would become:

SALES PRICE = (SALES PRICE × PRODUCTS SOLD) − QUANTITY DISCOUNT

the only problem being that quantity discounts are calculated on individual orders, not on the total of all orders. In that case Revenue would be the total of all order values after individual quantity discounts were taken into account.

Add to that the fact that Revenue is in itself a meaningless figure as profit is far more important and it could well be that the spreadsheet has to be extended to include the formula:

PROFIT = REVENUE − (FIXED COSTS + VARIABLE COSTS)

Another advantage of writing those calculations down in plain English is that they can then be checked to confirm that they are valid – that the stated calculation will produce the right result. Where the formula in question is a pre-defined industry standard, such as the method of calculating depreciation, this may be of only marginal benefit, but everything else must be checked thoroughly.

Given that Variable Costs are entirely dependent on the number of products sold, it becomes easy to see how even the simplest of spreadsheets can develop complications undreamt of at the beginning. Because of this, anyone about to build a spreadsheet must make sure that all formulas, calculations and relationships are decided and agreed in advance. If not, the spreadsheet will fail. At the risk of repetition, if the calculations cannot be expressed in simple terms or written down just as easily before the work begins, it will never happen when sitting in front of a computer.

Checking validity

The chances are any spreadsheet will contain some form of relationship between the various items of data which was first expressed formally when the spreadsheet was being designed. Thus it makes sense to confirm that those relationships are valid and that the calculations based on them actually work in practice. If not, there is every possibility that the spreadsheet will produce meaningless garbage with all that implies for any decisions based on the results of that spreadsheet.

The best way of checking these relationships is to take the extremes of any value and perform the calculations. For example, the time taken to travel a certain distance depends on the speed of the object being moved, which should hold true whether the object is at rest (zero speed) or travelling at the speed of light. However, if after performing the calculations there are obvious discrepancies, that can only mean the original formula was wrong. In other words, time to go back to the drawing board.

There is also every chance that a particular formula is based on more than just two figures calculated together. For example, the distance/speed formula above might also include any delays, which could be due to anything from traffic congestion to air friction, depending on the object being moved. If this is the case, the relationships between all factors involved must be thoroughly tested at the extreme edges where problems are generally more noticeable. For good measure a third calculation taking the mid-point of all values should also be performed so that the formula can be tested under all conditions. This might seem overly complex, but if this procedure is followed then when it comes to creating a spreadsheet there can be no doubt about its validity. Everything else is just implementation.

It is also a good idea to draw a rough map or diagram showing the exact relationship between each item of information so that when it comes to the actual building of the spreadsheet there is a clear understanding as to how everything fits together. As an illustration, the map of the Sales Revenue/Profit example would look something like Figure 1.1.

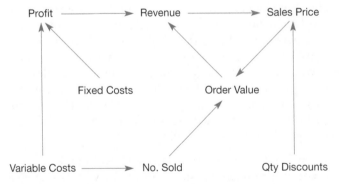

Figure 1.1 The map of the Sales Revenue/Profit example

It is simple to construct a map (or diagram), and this together with a formal statement of every formula being used can be of such immense value that the time spent doing it will be repaid many times over when the spreadsheet is being constructed.

There is still more to do before a computer is needed, but following this procedure means that, whatever other problems have to be faced, there will at least be a solid base to work from.

Once you have this foundation, you need to think about the data itself, its sources and its accuracy.

Data

As a spreadsheet exists solely to manipulate figures it follows that, unless those figures are accurate, building the spreadsheet becomes a pointless exercise. Once again that sounds obvious, but there are still many ways to go wrong even over something so basic.

The first pitfall concerns the accuracy of those figures, or that data. This is a major design consideration for the simple reason that it is useless trying to work to three decimals places if the original figures are little more than estimates rounded to the nearest thousand, or even million. In fact, if there are too many estimates involved, or even one which could have a significant effect on the overall results, the entire spreadsheet has to be treated with caution. This is because estimates are what is known as judgemental data: they depend entirely on individual judgement, not proven fact. Therefore, as the estimates can vary depending on the judgement of the people making them, the spreadsheet itself can never be wholly accurate. At best it can provide a rough and ready calculation, at worst it can be totally misleading.

Anyone faced with a situation like this would be better advised to make a computer model taking into account a range of estimates or at the very least use a scenario manager (for both of which see later).

Discrete or continuous?

It is also worth asking whether the figures being supplied are discrete or continuous. A discrete variable, or figure, is a measure of something that can exist only as a whole number. Examples here could be the number of units produced, the number of products sold or the number of people on a payroll. Alternatively, a continuous variable is a measure of anything that may have an upper and lower limit but could have any value in between. For example, measures of temperature, volume or humidity are all continuous.

This might not seem like much of a problem – after all, numbers representing degrees centigrade can be manipulated just as easily as a number representing workers on a production line – but there are differences and anyone constructing a spreadsheet should be aware of them. The first and most obvious is that while it is possible to have half a degree centigrade, there is no such thing as half a person or half a sale. Being discrete, these must increase or decrease in single whole units. Temperature, on the other hand, can vary between all possible fractions of a degree, limited only by the accuracy of the measuring equipment. More importantly, if the temperature was measured at intervals of, say, one degree, that could give a certain reading – yet an entirely different reading would be produced if the temperature was measured every half a degree, or five degrees.

It is this which causes the problem because when there is no clear unit of measurement, like whole people or whole sales, measurements can be purely arbitrary, even judgemental. In which case, like every other judgemental value, they have to be treated with extreme caution. You should ask questions such as why that unit of measurement was chosen in the first place, what would be the effect if it was changed, and what would happen if that variable was measured to a different degree of precision. As all of these can cause such profound changes to the accuracy and usefulness of the spreadsheet, anyone who has to deal with such continuous variables would be well advised to consider the implications involved in their use, if necessary taking advice from whoever provided the measurements.

Time series

There can be similar problems associated with what is known as the time series. As the name implies, this involves some form of measurement taken over a given period of time which can, unless checked, introduce just as many errors as continuous variables. Obviously there will be occasions when the time series is fixed – sales for the third quarter of a year will always be sales for the third quarter of that year – but just as often the time series involved can be judgemental; someone has decided the time scale over which a series of measurements should be taken.

The point is that anybody who wants to work with spreadsheets has to be aware of the problems that can be caused by differing measurements, or the difference between discrete and continuous variables. In fact, it all comes down to one simple question: just ask what the effect would be if the intervals between measurements, or the accuracy of those measurements, was changed. If the answer is none, the figures can be used as they are; otherwise they need further work. For example, if a particular measurement was taken every ten minutes, would the readings obtained be exactly double that of readings taken every five minutes? No matter how slight the difference, if it exists then so does the problem. How the problem is solved is, of course, a different question and one which can only be answered on an individual basis, but at least being aware of the problem is a major step towards solving it.

Consistency

Finally, also make sure that the data being entered is in consistent units of measurement. Even something as apparently simple as having one measurement expressed in hours and another expressed in minutes can introduce extra complexity as, somewhere, the one will have to be converted into the other. While multiplying or dividing by 60 might not seem like much of a problem, it will probably have to be done as part of a much larger formula where mistakes can be easily made, and which can be difficult to spot. If the data must be entered in this way it is best to set up an intermediate cell in the spreadsheet where the conversion is done and then use the value in that cell for further calculation within a more complex formula. Needless to say this also holds good for situations where more complex conversion factors are involved, such as metric and imperial weights and measures. Building spreadsheets can be complicated enough as it is; why add more complications unnecessarily?

Data is not always as spreadsheet-friendly as it could be. Despite its power and flexibility, the spreadsheet cannot produce viable results from unviable data, so be prepared to challenge a given set of figures and question the source.

Presentation

Like every other aspect of building a spreadsheet its final presentation must be carefully planned. Quite apart from the fact that it demonstrates a professional attitude, if the spreadsheet is difficult to understand its results will be disregarded for that very reason. As such, taking the time to decide how the data will be presented is always a good idea.

Spend some time studying various spreadsheets, decide on the good and bad points, find out how a particular effect was achieved or a particular calculation performed, then apply them to your own work. That way good design ideas are spread and mistakes are avoided.

The best place to find design ideas is in other spreadsheets. Whether it is the sample files that are included as standard by the spreadsheet manufacturers, or those created by others inside or outside the company, everyone has access to many spreadsheets.

It also helps if the results are stored in the part of the spreadsheet that first appears when it is opened. Nothing is worse than having to scroll through screen after screen of meaningless figures to find the results that explain it all.

The biggest mistake most people make is in getting too close to the figures. They rapidly become familiar with what are in practice just columns upon columns of numbers, to the extent that sometimes even column headings and sub-totals are irrelevant. They already know where to look to find the right figure. The problem is that no one else can do this and so to the rest of the world that spreadsheet remains impenetrable.

The first point is not to have data scattered all over the screen in whatever cell first came to hand. Instead, always keep the results separate from the data used to generate those results.

This not only makes a spreadsheet easier to understand but should it need to be printed out, you need only specify the small range of cells holding the data to be presented. The rest of the spreadsheet can be safely ignored.

Secrecy

At this point it is worth mentioning that there could be information on a spreadsheet which is not for general consumption. A customer might appreciate a report showing the material and equipment used on a particular job, but the sales mark-up and profit margin is still something to be kept secret. If both of these are on the spreadsheet, there are two distinct ways of dealing with the problem.

The first, and most obvious, is to store this confidential information somewhere else on the spreadsheet where it will never be printed out, assuming the proper design rules are followed. Although this would keep sensitive data off a print-out it would still be visible on a computer screen should anyone else use that particular spreadsheet, which may, in itself, be the cause of further problems. To prevent this it is possible to hide a particular cell or range of cells. The values in those cells can still be used for further calculation, but they will never appear on the screen.

The only drawback with this is that it is not so much a particular cell that is hidden but an entire column, so anything else in that column would be hidden and therefore out of reach – something that can be cured only by advance planning.

Design rules

If anything, this highlights what has to be one of the golden rules of design: decide what goes where and do it before using a computer. For simple spreadsheets a rough sketch will do, something to show what information will be in what cell, while for large, complex spreadsheets best practice is to break it down into separate modules. For example, to create a spreadsheet which included order processing, stock control and invoicing you would start by drawing a map showing the relationship between these modules, which could look something like that shown in Figure 1.2.

To find out how to do this refer to the manual; look under Cells – Hide.

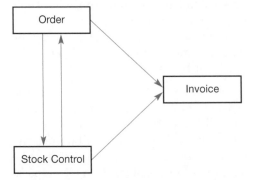

Figure 1.2 A map to show the relationship between modules

Here the Order module would hold such details as customer and products ordered, the Stock Control module would hold stock levels, with the Invoice module to calculate the amount charged for that order.

Although simplistic in the extreme, this does illustrate the principles involved. A map is drawn showing the relationship between the modules which can be followed by another map showing the relationship between the data in each of those modules, so what was at first a complex project becomes a collection of simple calculations. In practice, of course, this rough map would then need elaboration to show the titles of each data item (Part Number, Unit Price, etc) to help decide exactly what cells should be used, but that is not difficult.

Another advantage of this method is that by keeping the data separate it can also be printed out separately so that a stock report could be produced simply by printing out that range of cells while an invoice could be prepared just as easily.

Even without that it is still easy to see how spreadsheets, no matter what their complexity, can be constructed effortlessly. Armed with a map, or maps, showing the relationships between the data, clearly stated formulas describing the calculations, and the knowledge that those same formulas have been thoroughly checked, all that remains is to transfer it to a spreadsheet.

However, there are a few other points to consider. To begin with there is the question of along or down. Will the spreadsheet be extended to the next screen to the right, making it long and thin, or will the data go down to the screen below? To a certain extent the nature of the work being done will determine this and it could just as easily be both, but it is still a question that needs to be answered at the design stage. Apart from any other considerations it helps to determine where the data labels should go. This is a relevant point because as more data items are entered into the spreadsheet, so the data labels – the titles – will disappear off the screen. You can prevent this by fixing the top row, or left-most column, so that it stays in place on the screen no matter how far along or down the data is. The only problem is that the entire row or column will remain fixed, so if you are going to do this, it is best not to put data on the same row or column as data labels.

Similarly, if a cell width has to be changed – and the chances are that this will happen in every spreadsheet – every other cell in that column will also be changed. Cell widths cannot be changed individually. Unfortunately, as these cells are narrowed or widened, other cells could be forced off the edge of the screen or, conversely, cells could appear and give the spreadsheet a confused look. Even without that, columns of figures, each of varying width, look messy. The only way to avoid that is at the design stage, when such things can be taken into account.

Deciding whether to go along or down is really personal preference. Once the tradition was always to work down the spreadsheet, although that had nothing to do with good design practice but came about because that way used less computer memory at a time when computer memory (RAM) was a precious commodity. Nowadays even a standard computer comes supplied with so much RAM that it will never be a problem for spreadsheet users. Games use far more memory than a spreadsheet ever will.

Finally there are those elements of spreadsheet design which most people think of as coming under the heading of presentation: colour, typeface and overall looks.

A data label is just a jargon-filled way of describing the column or row headings. If a column has a heading of SALES and a series of figures underneath it, the figures representing sales are the data and the heading is the data label.

- Nothing does more to improve the appearance of a spreadsheet than colour and in the process makes it easier to read. In particular you should investigate the facility to print negative values in red.

- Three is the maximum number of typefaces recommended. Any more than that and the document starts to appear messy and ill-conceived.

- The overall look can be improved simply by drawing lines below certain totals, or certain results. Other than that, blank spaces between groups of figures can be highly effective. However, this has to be decided in advance.

Although all spreadsheets have the facility to insert extra rows or columns, in fact all the spreadsheet does is move all the cells containing data down by one row or across by one column. (For example, data that was once stored in cell G14 could then be stored in cell G15.) While this has the effect of creating a blank row, the spreadsheet cannot go through every formula in every cell and alter the reference to match the new location of that data – this has to be done by hand. For a large spreadsheet, not only would this be time consuming but if just one cell was left uncorrected the rest of the spreadsheet would be unworkable. In other words, spend a small amount of time at the beginning deciding what the spreadsheet should look like – or spend hours trying to discover why it will not work.

The case for good design is made. Now all it takes is to convert that design into a functioning spreadsheet.

Built-in functions

2

The order of precedence

Relative and absolute cell addressing

The pocket calculator

Formatting

Functions

Although there are many highly complex functions built into a modern spreadsheet, the best place to start is with those that are much easier both to use and to describe. Other than the fact that these are very often the building blocks of much larger spreadsheets, they can also be used to illustrate the concepts and terminology involved. Look on this chapter as a foundation course: the means by which the essentials can be understood before more advanced topics are introduced.

The basis of all functions is the mathematical operators which allow a spreadsheet to multiply, divide, add or subtract. These may seem simple, but they can cause more problems than any other function, all because of something known as the order of precedence.

The order of precedence

While traditional pencil and paper mathematics calculates the formula from left to right, performing whatever operation comes next in line, spreadsheets work differently. They give precedence to some mathematical operators over others according to pre-defined rules. This is known as the order of precedence, and follows the format:

- brackets
- multiplication and division
- addition and subtraction.

Any expression inside brackets will be calculated first, followed by any division or multiplication, with addition or subtraction being performed last. For example, 6+5*4 would, in pencil and paper terms, equal 44 (6+5 equals 11 then multiply by 4). However, since a spreadsheet always calculates the multiplication before the addition, it would return the answer of 26 (5*4 equals 20 plus 6). To get the result of 44, the first part of the formula would have to be written inside brackets to become (6+5)*4 which would give the correct result as that part of the formula inside the brackets would be calculated first. Similarly:

8–7*3	equals	–13	NOT	3
4+4/2	equals	6	NOT	4
(8+2)/2+8	equals	13	NOT	1

If nothing else this shows the problem involved. If you are still uncertain, try working through the above examples, if necessary entering them into a spreadsheet, until you understand how the answers were arrived at. It is no exaggeration to say that without a proper appreciation of the order of precedence, creating a valid spreadsheet is impossible.

Once you understand the order of precedence, it is time to consider some of the more esoteric functions which exist by the hundred. Some of the most common are illustrated in Figure 2.1.

Although by no means an attractive spreadsheet this does at least have the advantage that it can be created easily – which is something that should be done. With spreadsheets, as with any other activity, the route to competence is practice.

Start by entering the data labels in cells C3 and G3 followed by those in row 4. Then add the data in columns A5–A9, B5–B9, F5–F9 and G5–G9. (Ignore the

If you enter a formula without taking the order of precedence into account, there will be no warning messages. All that will happen is that the wrong answer will be derived from the formula – and it could be a long time before the mistake is spotted, if at all.

	A	B	C	D	E	F	G	H
1			Results For	November-01				
2								
3			Sold				Bought	
4	Product	Quantity	S.P	Value		Quantity	B.P.	Value
5	AAA	35	£29.38	£1,028.13		20	£23.50	£470.00
6	BBB	45	£57.19	£2,573.44		50	£45.75	£2,287.50
7	CCC	23	£26.56	£610.94		75	£21.25	£1,593.75
8	DDD	12	£32.19	£386.25		20	£25.75	£515.00
9	EEE	43	£22.00	£946.00		10	£17.60	£176.00
10								
11	Total	158	£167.31	£5,544.75		175	£133.85	£5,042.25
12								
13		Avg Sold	32			Margin	25.00%	
14		Avg Bought	35			Profit	£502.50	
15								

Figure 2.1 Some of the more esoteric functions of a spreadsheet

currency signs as they will be dealt with later, for the moment just enter the figures.) Finally add the data label in cell F13 and the data in cell G13 which should be entered as 0.25, not 25%. After that it is time to enter a formula.

In cell H5 the Value is obviously the quantity bought multiplied by the Buying Price (BP), which means the formula is:

```
=F5*G5
```

This takes the figure stored in cell F5 and multiplies it by the value stored in cell G5, placing the result in H5 which was the cell where the formula was entered.

That done, a similar formula has to be entered into cells H6–H9 which, in this case, can be done without further typing. Simply highlight both the cell holding the formula and the cells where that formula has to be copied to and then select Fill Down from the Edit menu. This works no matter what spreadsheet is used, although there are other ways of doing the same thing individual to each package. (Once again the help files or manual are a good place to look.)

After that it is time to consider the Selling Price (SP) which, for the purposes of this spreadsheet, has been defined as Buying Price plus 25%. To put that another way, the profit margin is 25%, which means the formula for cell C5 is:

    =G5*G13+G5

This takes the figure stored in cell G5 (the Buying Price), multiplies it by the value shown in G13 (the Margin), then adds the result to the value of G5 to produce a Selling Price 25% higher than the Buying Price.

Although apparently simple, this illustrates some essential points of spread-sheet design. Firstly, showing the profit margin in a separate cell means that if at any time that margin were to be changed, you would simply need to alter that one cell and the entire spreadsheet would be automatically recalculated. In this way anything subject to change, such as VAT, income tax or hourly wage rates, could be handled with a minimum of effort. Theoretically, of course, the formula for C5 could have been entered as G5*1.25, which would have given the same result, but a month or two down the line it might not be quite so obvious what that 1.25 referred to, or even why it was there. More importantly, a change in the profit margin would mean searching every individual cell to change the value by hand. In short, then, keeping values in separate cells and

The = sign tells the spreadsheet that F5 is a cell reference, not a data label. Several other signs can also be used, according to preference – these can be found in the manual or help files.

then referring to those cells in subsequent formulas not only makes the spreadsheet flexible, it also makes the formulas easier to understand, no matter how long ago they were created (assuming those values in the separate cells had data labels associated with them, naturally).

Intermediate cells

Closely associated with this is a concept known as intermediate cells. This means that rather than having one complex formula it is often better to have several simple formulas, each one showing intermediate stages in the final calculation. For example, in Figure 2.1 it would be perfectly possible to have one cell showing the profit of each product (Buying Price*Margin) and then refer to that cell in the final calculation of the Selling Price (Buying Price+Profit).

For formulas where there is even the slightest degree of complexity this should be considered not so much recommended as mandatory, in the initial stages at least. Later, once the spreadsheet is operational and the logic has been proven, the formulas in the various intermediate cells can be combined to create just the one formula without any intermediate steps, but until then always show them. That way any problem with the logic or the functioning of a spreadsheet can be solved without the added complication of a complex formula being incorrectly entered and so producing the wrong result. In a large spreadsheet there are any number of reasons why it might not work first time; keeping the formulas simple to begin with means there is less to worry about.

However, there is at least now a formula entered into cell C5 and it would be reasonable to assume that this could then be copied down the column. Reasonable, but wrong. In this particular case things are slightly complicated by the presence in the formula of cell G13 – that and a procedure known as relative and absolute cell addressing.

Relative and absolute cell addressing

There are times when the address of a particular cell is relative only to the cell that holds the formula containing that address. For example, if the formula in, say, H5 is =G5*3, then the formula in H5 is relative to G5. However, if that formula was then copied into H6, it would have to be changed to read =G6*3.(Obviously this assumes that column G was a list of individual values that had to be multiplied by three.) While this is so fundamental to the process of copying cells that the spreadsheet handles the conversion automatically, nevertheless there are times when something else is required – when the address of a cell must be absolute.

In Figure 2.1 the cell G13 holds the value of the profit margin and is used in formulas such as =G5*G13+G5 which can be found in cell C5. Unfortunately, if that formula was simply copied to the row beneath it would read =G6*G14+G6 because the spreadsheet would move all the addresses down by one row. This is where the problem begins as, no matter where that formula is copied to, it must still show the address G13. To make matters worse, cell G14 is a blank cell which the spreadsheet would interpret as being zero and so in place of the profit margin it would multiply the Buying Price by zero – a mistake easy to spot in this spreadsheet, but likely to be a lot harder to find in something more complex.

What is needed, then, is a way of telling the spreadsheet that the reference to cell G13 must remain unchanged (absolute) even though all the other cell references in that formula can change relative to the row the formula is in. The good news is that this can be done easily enough.

All you need to do is place a '$' sign in front of any cell reference which is to remain fixed (absolute) and the rest happens automatically. The only slight complication is that both the row and the column reference must be treated separately as it is possible to have one relative and the other absolute. That means the column reference could be fixed while the row reference changes as the formula is copied or, alternatively, the column could change and the row could be fixed. Either way is possible and the process is identical.

The first way of doing it is to simply include the '$' sign when the cell reference' is being entered into a formula, while the other way is to place the cursor over a cell reference already included in a formula and then press F4. That works for all spreadsheets. Not only that, but pressing F4 again will cycle through all the available options until the right one appears, at which point simply press Enter and the job is done.

If anyone is still confused about absolute and relative cell addressing, the best advice is to enter the formula into C5 without the '$' sign, copy it into the other cells and see what happens. After that, try changing the column or row reference into an absolute; copy it again, which overwrites the original formula, and see what effect that has.

Therefore the options are:

- $G$4 – both column and row references are fixed (absolute);
- $G4 – the column reference is fixed but the row is not;
- G$4 – the row reference is fixed but not the column.

To return to the spreadsheet, the formula in C5 should be changed to read:

    =G5*G$13+G5

This fixes the row reference and leaves the column reference relative as this will not change when the formula is copied down into other cells (although it would do no harm to also make it absolute). After that, of course, this formula should be copied down into the relevant cells.

Once the formula, complete with absolute cell references, has been entered and copied, the next step is simple. In cell D5 enter the formula:

```
=B5*C5
```

Copy this into the cells below and it is time to make use of the most valuable tool of all when creating spreadsheets: the pocket calculator.

The pocket calculator

There are any number of reasons why a formula might return an incorrect result:

- the order of precedence could be wrong;
- wrong cell references might have been entered by mistake;
- there could be problems with the formula itself.

For these and many other reasons the results should be checked, which is best done with a pocket calculator. In that way any potential problems can be found at an early stage when correction is easier and before the results of that spreadsheet are used to take what could be far-reaching decisions.

In the case of this spreadsheet the calculations are simple enough to make it obvious if any mistakes have been made, but even so the results should still be checked. Good working practice should become a habit. Needless to say, not every single calculation has to be confirmed. All it takes is one or two checks at key points along the way. To begin with, look at any cell where a formula has been entered (like C5 in this spreadsheet) and use a calculator to work out what the answer should be, taking the actual figures as shown in the spreadsheet. If both calculator and spreadsheet give the same answer, there is no problem; if not, find out where the mistake is and correct it. After that, if the formula has been copied into other cells, select one or preferably two and repeat the process with the calculator.

Now all it takes is to show the totals. In cell A11 add the data label. There are some spreadsheets which automatically sum the contents of all non-blank columns to the right of the word 'Total' whenever it is entered into a spreadsheet, so it could be that a figure has already appeared in cells B11, C11 and D11. If it has, there is still more work to do as the summing process would have stopped at column E, a blank column. To put that another way, whether a spreadsheet includes this particular facility or not, other ways of adding up a row of figures still have to be found.

One way is to use the built-in function known as SUM (or @SUM depending on the spreadsheet). This function, like all the functions, can be accessed either through the menu system or from an icon at the top of the screen. Using it, no matter what the spreadsheet, will take the form of SUM(Range) where (Range) is the cells that are to be totalled. Here you highlight the appropriate cells with the mouse and then press Enter. The total is now included in the spreadsheet.

As an alternative, look at the row of icons at the top of the screen which is known as the Toolbar or the Speedbar depending on the spreadsheet. One of these icons will have some picture or sign that denotes addition, or the symbol 'Σ' which is a mathematical sign meaning the sum of. Once you have found this place the cursor in the cell where the total is to be shown, click on the icon and a range of cells will be automatically highlighted. Assuming these are the cells to be totalled, press Enter; if not, highlight the correct cells and then press Enter. Either way the job is then done.

Given that cells B11, C11, D11, F11, G11 and H11 all have to be totalled, try using a different method in each case if for no other reason than to gain experience in using them all. They all have their place in spreadsheet construction, so you should try them all.

Formatting

Now that the spreadsheet is starting to take shape, it might be a good time to show that some of those figures are in fact money. First highlight the range of cells concerned which in this case is C5 to D11.

What happens after that depends on the spreadsheet; some have a menu option of Range followed by Properties, while others have a menu option of Format followed by Range. Either way you will be presented with another list of choices, of which one will be Currency, or Number followed by Currency. Select that and the spreadsheet will automatically change to show just two digits to the right of the decimal point and with the '£' in place. Then do the same for the range G5 to H11 and the job is done. It is that simple, especially when some spreadsheets have the currency option set up as an icon at the top of the screen.

Even so, there is still a lot more to the business of formatting a range of cells. There are many more options apart from currency, the two most popular of which are Percentage and Number.

In spreadsheet terminology any group of adjacent cells which are to be treated in the same way is known as a range.

An alternative in some spreadsheets is to highlight the range and then right-click the mouse. This will bring up a menu with Format as one of the options.

This multiplication by 100 can cause confusion, or worse, if the original figure has been entered wrongly, as the simple act of formatting will then produce errors on a gigantic scale.

Percentage

The percentage option does more than just add the '%' sign to a number. It also multiplies that number by 100. This was why the percentage profit margin in G13 had to be entered as 0.25. When the cell is formatted as a percentage (and now is as good a time as any to do this), it will then be changed to show 25%. However, if the figure originally entered was 25, then formatting the cell would have produced a highly lucrative profit margin of 2,500% – and the rest of the spreadsheet would have been calculated on that basis.

Number

In most cases the formatting of numbers is deciding how many decimal places to show. While this may not always be an issue, there are times when spreadsheets work to just too many decimals places for the results to be sensible. An obvious example here would be when the figures being entered are no more than estimates rounded to the nearest thousand, or even million. As no one needs calculations based on such estimates to be correct to six decimal places, a more credible display would be to show the results formatted to just one or even zero places.

Changing the number format is easy. Anyone who has followed the menu option for currency or percentage just has to make a different selection. Even so, there are still pitfalls, which can best be explained by a simple demonstration.

Format three cells to show zero decimal places. In the first two enter the figure 2.4 and in the third calculate the total of the other two. Do it right and the first two cells will show the figure 2 and the third will prove that 2 + 2 = 5. So what went wrong?

When the figure 2.4 was entered, the spreadsheet rounded this down to 2. However, it was only the display of the number that was altered. The spreadsheet still worked to the original figure, as proved when it calculated the total. Being 4.8, this was rounded to 5, which was the number displayed. A cheap trick it might be, but it does illustrate a fundamental problem.

As this example demonstrates, if the formatting option is chosen it is easily possible for the spreadsheet to produce ridiculous-looking numbers and, to make matters worse, in a large spreadsheet trying to find the source of the mistake will be close to impossible. In this case not even using a calculator will help as in all probability the numbers you are entering into the calculator will be as they appear on the screen and not as they are being used by the spreadsheet. To try to use the actual figures would show the problem, but it would be time consuming and even then you would be nowhere near solving the problem. To do that calls for a function.

When a cell is formatted to a particular number of decimal places it is only the display of that figure which is altered. The underlying figure is still stored and used in all spreadsheet calculations.

Functions

To begin with an example, select the function ROUND (or @ROUND). This takes the form of ROUND(n,x) where n is the number to be considered and x is the number of decimal places the spreadsheet should work to. The difference is that this function forces the spreadsheet to actually work to a specified degree of accuracy, instead of just displaying the result to that specified degree, and so the problem of ridiculous figures never arises. As proof, take three more blank cells and in the first two enter the formula:

```
=ROUND(2.4,0)
```

When these are totalled, the answer will be displayed, correctly, as 4.

To see how that works in the spreadsheet first enter the data labels in cells B13 and B14 and then in cell C13 start by using a different function: Average (or @AVG). Unsurprisingly this function calculates the average value of a given range and so, again unsurprisingly, that range must be specified, which is done in exactly the same way as for the SUM function. Hit the Enter key and use a calculator to confirm that the result is correct. Assuming it is, the formula should then be edited to read:

```
=ROUND(AVERAGE(B5:B9),0)
```

When this is also done for cell C14 using the range F5:F9, the result will appear as shown in Figure 2.1.

Apart from producing the desired result, this introduces several of the elements that go towards the use of any built-in function. In strict order these are:

- **brackets** – a function encloses what are known as its arguments inside brackets to set them apart from any other figures or cell references contained in the formula;

- **arguments** – the part of a function where cell references or other criteria, such as the number of decimal places to be used, are referred to as its argument;

- **separators** – where a function has more than one argument, a semi-colon or comma is used to separate them so that the spreadsheet knows where one ends and the other begins.

In the formula above the function which calculates the averages is itself the argument for the function which rounds the figure to a set number of decimal places. It is this ability to incorporate functions within functions that gives spreadsheets their immense power and flexibility. All it takes is the knowledge just gained – that and an easy-to-acquire ability to manipulate functions like the building blocks they really are.

To make it even easier there are very few ways of going wrong, of which the easiest, and most common, is to misplace the brackets around each of the function's arguments. As even the relatively simple formula above shows, there can sometimes be a confusing number of brackets involved which must all be in the correct place. If not, the spreadsheet will return an error message and while it might try to indicate the source of that error it is unlikely to be successful. All it can really do is point to the place where the logic of that formula breaks down. Then you usually need to go back to first principles and check every single aspect of what could be a long and complex formula.

However, there is one simple check which you can do. Just count the number of brackets. If those facing one way '(' are unequal to those facing the other ')' then the cause of the problem is obvious. Work out where the missing bracket should go and the chances are that the formula will work. Nevertheless, deciding where that bracket should go is not always straightforward, especially in a long formula.

The best idea is to slowly build up the formula step by step. Start with a simple formula or function, check to see whether it works, then add the next function and make sure that works before adding the next. In this way the formula can be confirmed at each stage of its construction.

Another common mistake is to use what are known as circular references. For example, if the formula in cell F7 includes the value stored in G7 while the value in G7 depended on the result of the formula in F7, it would be impossible for that formula to work. Its reference would be circular. While that may seem obvious in such a simple example, in practice the circular reference could involve several cells which would make it that much harder to track down. Under those circumstances the best way is to go back to the map which should have been drawn before the spreadsheet was even started. The cause of the problem will lie in there.

Any other problems are most likely to relate to the way a particular function operates. For example, if a function is asked to perform a calculation on a range of cells, the results could be different than expected depending on whether or not that range contained any blank cells. In some cases they will be ignored while in others they will be taken into account. This is something you can determine only by reading the manual or help files. Failing that, the judicious use of a calculator should at least bring the problem to light.

IF

Probably the most useful, not to mention the most widely used, of all the functions is IF. To see this in action on the spreadsheet, in cell G14 enter the formula:

```
=D11-H11
```

As should be obvious, this takes the value of goods sold and subtracts the value of goods bought to show the amount of profit made (which means the cell should also be formatted for currency). Assuming a profit has been made, this is all straightforward, but if a loss was made the data label beside the figure should reflect that. In other words, the data label should say Profit when money was made and Loss when money was lost. One way of doing this might be to perform the calculation and then type the data label depending on the result, although a much better idea is to automate the entire procedure, which is where the IF (or @IF) function comes into its own.

The function itself takes the form of IF(criteria; action if true; action if false). The criteria is some form of test which the spreadsheet makes on a specified cell or cells. In plain English that test could be something like 'IF income is greater than outgoings' or 'IF exports are greater than imports'. Obviously the appropriate cell references would be used instead of those statements, but the test can be as simple or as complicated as the demands of the spreadsheet call for. If need be, the criteria could include an entire formula complete with its own functions. Anything is possible.

The actions tell the spreadsheet what to do if the criteria is satisfied, if the conditions are met. The first action is performed if the condition is met; the second action is performed if not. In the terminology of spreadsheets, if the criteria evaluates as true, the first action is performed, and the second action is performed if the criteria evaluates as false.

In the spreadsheet this means the formula to be entered into cell F14 should be:

```
=IF(D11>=H11,"Profit","Loss")
```

Here the criteria is to see if D11 (Sold) is greater than H11 (Bought). To be slightly more accurate it also tests to see whether the two are equal, which accounts for the symbol '>' which signifies greater than, while '=' obviously means equal. Put together '>=' means greater than or equal to in the same way that '<=' means less than or equal to. In the world of spreadsheets these combined symbols appear frequently, or at least they should, assuming the formula has been carefully designed.

With so many functions now available nobody can be fully conversant with them all. At best you can know a few, leaving all the others to be discovered as and when required. For the same reason no book, other than the manual, can even begin to cover how each one should be used. All that can be done is to establish the general principles and leave the rest to help files and common sense.

In the above formula it would have been just as easy to write D11>H11 (D11 greater than H11), which would work right up to the time when events conspired to make the two equal. What would happen then would depend entirely on how the spreadsheet handles such an event, which is exactly the point: the result of that formula is no longer in the hands of whoever created it. That might not seem like much of a problem in this example where the chances of the two being equal are slim, to put it mildly, but on other occasions the chances could be higher and so the problem becomes greater. While it could be ignored, and might never become an issue, a much more sensible approach is to simply add that final '=' sign so there is no danger of losing control. The test performed by the spreadsheet will always do exactly what is expected no matter what the circumstances.

What will happen after the test has been performed depends entirely on the next part of the function's argument. As already explained, assuming the condition has been satisfied (the criteria evaluates as true), the first action will be performed which in this case means showing the data label 'Profit'. The spreadsheet knows to treat this as a word – a text string in the jargon – because it has been enclosed in quote marks (''). Without those it would assume the argument was a cell reference, which in a different spreadsheet it could well be.

Any formula, no matter how complex, could be included in the knowledge that the calculation would be performed only if a certain specified condition was met. Similarly, the second action, which again could be a complex formula, would be performed only if the condition was not satisfied. As far as this spreadsheet is concerned, of course, that would mean showing the data label 'Loss'.

Once broken down into its constituent arguments no one could say the IF function was difficult to use. All it takes is the confidence to try – so try it. Enter the formula as shown and then experiment by changing the quantities of goods bought and sold until profit turns into a loss and the data label changes accordingly. Even in such a simple implementation the power of the function can be seen, not to mention its usefulness.

On a more mundane level it also comes close to finishing the spreadsheet. Almost, but not quite. There is still one more function to be considered. This is in cell D1, alongside its data label in cell C1, which seems to show nothing more than the date. But it does, in a very special way.

Some spreadsheets automatically format the cell for date when the NOW function is used, but even then the right date format will still have to be selected.

NOW

The function in question is NOW (or @NOW) which has no associated arguments. Nevertheless it should still be entered into cell D1, at which point the cell could contain a very large number. Ignoring what this number means for the moment, format the cell for date and from the choices offered choose whatever will display just the month and year.

Not only will the spreadsheet show the current month and year, but every time that spreadsheet is used it will always show whatever date is current. In this way, if a spreadsheet was designed to produce a monthly report, simply opening it would be enough to show what month the report was for.

As a concept that seems simple and yet it also opens the door to several other factors, all of which have a bearing on the way spreadsheets are designed and used.

Spreadsheets store dates as a series of consecutive numbers so that January 1st 1900 is day 0, January 2nd is day 1 and so on, right through to the massive numbers which correspond to the present day. In fact the hours, minutes and seconds of each day are stored as a decimal fraction of that number, which gives spreadsheets the ability to calculate dates to the exact second for any time in the past, present or future. By treating the date as a number spreadsheets, which were designed purely to manipulate numbers, can perform calculations based on times and dates. This adds greatly to their power and flexibility, especially when formatting a cell for date automatically converts that number into whatever date it represents.

Of course, if the date is stored as a number and all numbers can be manipulated by spreadsheets, it follows that the date shown can be equally manipulated. This can help with the problem of creating a report on a monthly basis: the report is always created in the following month. The August report would be created in September, the October report in November. How, then, can a spreadsheet reflect that fact if it has been set up to show the current month instead of the month preceding it? The answer is simple: change the formula.

An easy, if slightly crude, method would be to tell the spreadsheet to show the date 30 days before that which is current. This would be done using the formula:

```
=NOW()-30
```

As the cell is formatted to show just the month rather than the exact day of that month, this would work and in some spreadsheets nothing else is available. However, for those using Lotus 123 the function @NEXTMONTH should be considered as its arguments are the date and a number to show how many months forward or back it should show. Used here it would give a formula of:

```
@NEXTMONTH(@NOW(),-1)
```

The @NOW part of the argument would return the present date, with the second argument (−1) telling it to show the date one month earlier than present.

Unfortunately Excel has no NEXTMONTH function which means a little bit of creativity needs to be used. Here the first function to be used is DATE, which has as its arguments, year, month and day. For example, DATE(2001;9;7) would return a date of September 7th 2001. While this function can be useful in itself, for the purposes of the current spreadsheet it needs more work, beginning with a not very well-known option of the function. If a zero is entered as the date part of the argument, the function returns the last day of the previous month. In the example above, entering DATE(2001;9;0) would return the last day of August. Assuming the cell was then formatted to show just month and year, that would do the trick − except the date still has to be entered manually. To make the spreadsheet do all the work, a little bit more is needed.

As already mentioned, the NOW() function returns a number corresponding to the date, so what is needed is a way of converting that number into a format the DATE function can use. In other words the MONTH function is needed. As this returns the month number corresponding to the serial number, the formula MONTH(NOW()) would return the number 6 for June, 11 for November, and so on. Similarly, the YEAR function would return just the year, ie 2000, 2001, etc. These numbers can then be used in the DATE function.

Putting all of this together means that to automatically calculate the date of a previous month in Excel the formula to be used is:

```
=DATE(YEAR(NOW();MONTH(NOW());0)
```

A template might best be described as a skeleton spreadsheet. It will have the formulas, the functions and even the formatting, but no data. The idea is that a spreadsheet, such as that for a monthly report, could be created and then stored minus its data as a template. Then each month the template could be called up, the data entered, and the whole thing saved under an appropriate name. As the formulas were already in place, the spreadsheet would perform the correct calculations, with the added bonus that the following month the same

Templates

As we can see, dates and times represent no more problems than numbers when it comes to working with spreadsheets. All it takes is a proper understanding of the underlying principles and anything is possible. Even so, it does raise the question of why spreadsheets should be designed to automatically show the current date when it could be entered manually with very little typing. Here the answer is not to do with saving any effort but because of a template.

Converting a spreadsheet into a template is also simplicity itself. Just remove the data and then use the Save As option from the File menu. Select the file type from the dialog box that appears. In this case the file type should, naturally, be Template, or .XLT in Excel. Users of Lotus 123 should note that a special file has to be loaded first which must be done before working on the spreadsheet.

It is that simple – provided that a few, equally simple, rules are followed:

■ remove any empty worksheets before saving the spreadsheet as a template or else the empty sheets will be included in the template;

■ use the delete key to remove any numerical data before saving as this preserves any special formatting applied to the cells;

■ lock (or protect) the entire spreadsheet and then unlock (or unprotect) just those cells where data is to be entered. This prevents the spreadsheet being changed accidentally.

All spreadsheets come with a selection of pre-designed templates which may or may not be of any use but which should always be studied. These templates were created by professionals and so the design effects and use of functions are guaranteed to be of a high standard. And where better to find ideas and worked examples of functions that could then be incorporated into other spreadsheets?

Examining templates will also show you just how easy it is to create top-quality spreadsheets, something this chapter should also have made clear. There are many more functions to be considered, and many more techniques to be discussed, but at least you should now understand the basics, which is always a good place to start.

Continued

template could be called up and the process repeated. In this way the work of creating a spreadsheet would only have to be done once and yet it could be used over and over again.

Lookup tables and databases

3

Lookup tables

Databases

Data sources

While all the functions we have covered so far have involved the manipulation of figures in some way, there are also functions which allow data to be stored within a spreadsheet for later retrieval. This so greatly increases both the power of a spreadsheet and the range of applications over which it can be used that no one who aspires to competence can afford to ignore them.

These functions fall into two basic categories:

- lookup tables
- databases.

Both work differently and both are suitable for a different range of circumstances, which is why they are treated separately here, but that does not mean they need to be kept separate. In the real world, with the right application both could quite easily exist in the same spreadsheet.

Lookup tables

Of the two this is the most widely used. It is also the most flexible as there are, in fact, two functions, both of which involve looking up data in tables: vertical lookup and horizontal lookup. As their names imply, they operate in slightly different ways, but the principles are the same so they can be explained in the same way.

As we have said, the whole point of these functions is to look up data in tables, and the implementation is easy as all lookup functions take the form of:

    LOOKUP(Value,Range,Offset)

Here Value is the data to be searched for, which could be either a number or a word. Range is the group of cells which store the data table, and Offset is the number of rows along or down which the spreadsheet then moves so the answer can be returned. (The terminology will vary from spreadsheet to spreadsheet, but it will mean the same.)

Table 3.1 Sales per product for four geographical regions

PRODUCT	NORTH	SOUTH	EAST	WEST
AAA	5,000	6,200	3,400	4,200
BBB	2,100	3,200	1,900	4,700
CCC	6,200	2,700	5,100	1,900

Consider Table 3.1, which could be a table showing sales per product for each of the four geographical regions. Assuming it has already been entered into a spreadsheet and the range of cells holding that table has been given the name 'Sales', then to look up a particular value in the table, for example sales of product BBB in the Southern region, the formula could be entered as:

```
=VLOOKUP(BBB,Sales,2)
```

This works by making the spreadsheet look down the first column of the range Sales until it comes to the reference BBB. It would then move two columns along and return the answer 3,200. The reason the spreadsheet first looked

VLOOKUP searches down the first column of a range while HLOOKUP searches along the first row.

Individual cells can be named and that name used in place of the cell reference, which can make for easily understandable formulas. Sales*Price will always be more intelligible than J35*M56.

down the column was because the function used was VLOOKUP which means vertical lookup. Had horizontal or HLOOKUP been used, the formula would need to be:

=HLOOKUP(SOUTH,Sales,2)

This would search along the first row of the Sales range until it came to the reference SOUTH, then it would move down two rows to return the same 3,200 as before.

There are other aspects of both functions:

- A cell reference could be used as the value to be searched for, so entering a value into that cell would produce a different search result without having to change the formula.

- A cell reference could be used in place of the number of columns or rows to move along or down.

- Either of the arguments could be a formula in their own right, if necessary including another lookup function to search a different lookup table.

- The answer returned by a lookup function could itself be used as the basis for further calculations.

Naming cells

To name a range of cells, highlight the range in question, remembering to include the titles in the first row or column, then select 'Name' from the menu. A dialog box will appear for you to enter your chosen name.

If a range name is to be entered directly into a formula, either in a lookup function or anywhere else, it is also a good idea to give it an absolute reference.
That way the formula or function can be safely copied into other cells
(although in some spreadsheets this will not be necessary). In the example
above this would mean the formula to be entered should have been:

```
=VLOOKUP(BBB,$Sales,2)
```

(When the range is first being named do not include the '$' sign. It is needed
only in the formula and would cause confusion if it appeared anywhere else.)

Finally, if that first column or row to be searched contained only numbers, and
if those numbers were entered in strict ascending order, the value to be
searched for would not need to match exactly any of the numbers in the table.
Instead the search would stop at the entry closest to, but less than, the search
value. For example:

1.0	1.5	2.0	2.5	3.0	3.5
A	B	C	D	E	F

Here assume that the top row was for parcel weights and the second showed
which pricing band was associated with those weights. Also assume that the
range was given the name 'Weights' and that the formula entered into another
cell was:

```
=HLOOKUP(2.3,Weights,1)
```

If words are involved, if the value to be searched for is a word, not a number, the search will stop at the last entry in the table, then move down the column, or along the row, the specified number of steps to return the value there. This could be a problem if the initial search term is misspelled, so be careful about the words being used as table entries: make them easy to spell.

As there is no entry in the table for a weight of 2.3, the search would stop at 2.0 and return the value of C. If need be, of course, that value of C could then be used as a search value in another lookup table to return the cost of postage associated with that pricing band. In fact the entire process could be built into a single formula.

Case sensitive

The LOOKUP functions are also case sensitive, which means they would treat a word entered in capitals (upper case) as different to a word entered in normal letter (lower case) or even to a word where both were used. That means they would consider SOUTH, South and south as three different words, and yet as only one of these would be the correct term as entered in the lookup table, it follows that the other two would not be found. The spreadsheet would simply return the last value in the table, which has obvious implications for the correct functioning of the spreadsheet.

To avoid this always use upper case (capitals) when entering words into the lookup table, then amend the lookup formula slightly to include the function UPPER. For example:

```
=HLOOKUP(UPPER(B2),$Sales,2)
```

Assuming the word 'south' was entered into cell B2, the UPPER function would convert that into capitals (upper case) so the LOOKUP function would search the lookup table for the word 'SOUTH', which would happen no matter how the word was entered into cell B2. It may be *slightly* more complex but it does avoid a potential problem at source which can only be good design practice.

Spreadsheet practice

All of this might seem confusing, but everything should start to make sense once those lookup functions are used in practice, which means it is time to start work on another spreadsheet (Figure 3.1).

	A	B	C	D	E	F
1			INVOICE			
2						
3	Start date	05/11/1999			VAT Rate	17.50%
4	End date	07/11/1999			Labour	£50.00
5						
6						
7	Part No.	Description	Qty	Unit Price	Value	VAT
8	AB1234	Flange	2	£17.95	£35.90	£6.28
9	Cd2345	Cover	1	£21.45	£21.45	£3.75
10	gh4567	Handbook	1	£8.75	£8.75	£0.00
11						
12						
13						
14						
15						
16				Total Parts	£66.10	
17		Days Worked		Labour	£100.00	
18		2		VAT	£10.04	
19				Transport	£5.00	
20						
21				Total	£181.14	
22						

Figure 3.1 Working with the lookup functions

To begin with the title, every spreadsheet has the facility to do something like this, so experiment a bit. Enter the word, format it to a different size and perhaps change the typeface as well. This is not difficult but it can improve the presentation vastly.

After that you can do some real work, starting with the data labels in cells A3 and A4 and, for good measure, those in A7–F7. Now consider the dates shown in B3 and B4. Entering dates is easy: just type in the numbers as they appear complete with the backslash (/) to separate the days, months and years. Remember, though, to include all three, otherwise the spreadsheet will interpret two numbers separated by a backslash as a command to divide one number by the other. Once this date has been accepted, you can format it in any way you like.

Doing calculations involving dates is also easy. In cell B17 enter the data label, then underneath that (B18) enter the formula:

    =B4–B3

All this does is subtract one date from another to give the answer 2. In some spreadsheets this may be shown as a date because the cell will have been automatically formatted, but if so simply change the format. Instead of Date choose Number and, to keep things simple, set it to zero decimal places. Even though this part of the spreadsheet was included only as an exercise in calculations involving dates, it still makes the point – there is nothing difficult in entering and using dates.

Now it is time to start working on the lookup table proper, by entering the data shown on Figure 3.2.

	A	B	C	D
32	Part No.	Description	Unit Price	VAT
33	AB1234	Flange	17.95	1
34	CD2345	Cover	21.45	1
35	EF3456	Bracket	7.63	1
36	GH4567	Handbook	8.75	0
37	IJ5678	Mounting	6.25	1

Figure 3.2 Data for the lookup table

Once this is entered, highlight the range A32–D37 and title it Stock. This is all it takes to create a lookup table which you can then use.

As we know, the purpose of the lookup function is to search a data table according to specified criteria and then return a value from that table, also according to specified criteria. Here this means a spreadsheet where entering a part number into one cell will automatically return its description and unit price. Because of all the constraints mentioned earlier, and a few more yet to be considered, this means the formulas will start to become long and seemingly complex, but there will be nothing too difficult. As always the trick is to build the formula one step at a time.

The first formula will tell the spreadsheet to search the lookup table for the part number entered into cell A8 and then move sufficient columns along to return its description. So, enter the part number shown in A8 to give the function something to work with and then in cell B8 enter the formula:

```
=VLOOKUP(A8,Stock,2)
```

As well as different terminology, the various spreadsheets use a different numbering system for calculating the number of columns to move. With some, telling the spreadsheet to move one column along means look at the first column in the list, the column which has just been searched. For those spreadsheets the number 2 has to be entered into the formula to make it look at the next column along, while for other spreadsheets entering the figure 1 will make it move to the next column across. You can find out how this works for an individual spreadsheet by trial and error or by reading the manual, but if the above formula has returned something other than the matching description, then change the final argument of the function to 1. That should cure the problem.

In addition, do not forget the matter of upper or lower case entries, and change the formula to:

```
=LOOKUP(UPPER(A8),Stock,2)
```

This should make no difference as the part number shown in A8 was already in upper case. It is only when the next few part numbers are entered in lower case or a mixture of the two that the effect will be seen, but before doing that you should complete the row by entering a few more formulas. In C8 enter the quantity (2) and then in D8 enter the formula:

```
=LOOKUP(UPPER(A8),Stock,3)
```

This will return the unit price, which means the next cell, Value, is obviously unit price multiplied by quantity to give a formula of:

```
=C8*D8
```

After that things start to get slightly more complicated as the VAT has to be calculated, but this can be done by a simple trick. In the lookup table the VAT column shows only 1 or, in the case of the handbook, 0 and it is this which makes the trick work. To see it in action, enter the VAT rate in cell F3 (remember to enter it as 0.175 and then format for percentage). After that in cell F8 enter the formula:

```
=LOOKUP(UPPER(A8),Stock,4)*E8*F3
```

By way of an exercise, try working out what this formula will do before reading the explanation.

In this particular instance it will return the value shown in the VAT column of the lookup table (1) which will then be multiplied by the value of goods bought to produce exactly the same figure (1*£35.90=£35.90). This will then be multiplied by the VAT rate in F3 to give the amount due. So far this is all relatively straightforward; long-winded, but straightforward. However, the reason for doing it this way is to cater for the fact that some goods are zero rated, like the handbook in the lookup table. Here the figure first returned by the lookup function will be zero so, as zero multiplied by any figure is always zero, the VAT due will be shown to be exactly that: zero. Once explained the trick is simple, but immensely useful nevertheless.

The next step is to format the relevant cells for currency and then, just to see how all of this works in practice, try changing the part number or the quantity and watch everything else happen automatically. Sometimes this can be worth doing if only for the feeling of satisfaction, or power, that comes when everything works as it should.

By now it should also be obvious how the completed spreadsheet is supposed to work. Part numbers and quantities will be entered and the spreadsheet will then fill in the blanks, including the totals, to complete the invoice. In theory that sounds straightforward, but there is at least one more problem to consider: when those formulas just entered are copied down into the cells, below every single one of them will be an error message. There must be: there is no entry in the Part Number column for the lookup function to search for. When a part number is entered, the error messages will disappear and the formulas will be seen to work, but until then no one could expect that spreadsheet to be taken seriously – not with error messages all over it.

What is needed, then, is some way of keeping those cells blank even though the formulas will still be there waiting for a part number to be entered. In short, a test must be performed. If a part number is entered, the formula will go into action, but if not the cell must be kept blank and free of error messages.

The function needed here is IF. The first part of the function, the test, is to see whether anything has been entered into a particular cell. If the cell is blank, any spreadsheet will consider the value of that cell to be zero, which is how the test can be performed. In the spreadsheet here the test will be:

```
=IF(A8=0,Action if True,Action if False)
```

From there it becomes easy to see that if it is in fact zero, something has to happen to prevent the error message appearing. Again this can be done by a very useful trick. Simply enter a space between quote marks as the action if true. The spreadsheet will interpret this as a piece of text and will work on that basis, so the formula so far is:

```
=IF(A8=0," ",Action if False)
```

After that the action if false is, of course, the lookup function, which means that the entire formula for cell B8 is:

```
=IF(A8=0," ",VLOOKUP(UPPER(A8),Stock,2))
```

To recap. If a cell (in this case A8) is blank, the spreadsheet will assign it a value of zero. When that happens the IF function, which tests for exactly that, will show a space, although if that seems confusing try using a letter instead. For example, if the letter B, for blank, was substituted for the space, then every time A8 was blank B8 would show the letter B. Once you understand the principle, go back to using the space as that makes the trick work. The space cannot be seen so it looks as if the cell is blank and thus keeps the spreadsheet neat and free of error messages. Of course, if a part number is entered into A8 then the action if false is performed and the lookup function goes into action exactly as before.

This is probably better understood when it is seen in action so to begin, change all the formulas where necessary, meaning that D8 becomes:

```
=IF(C8=0," ",VLOOKUP(UPPER(A8),Stock,3))
```

Here the test is on C8, not A8, just to keep everything looking neat until the quantity is entered. Similarly, cell F8 becomes:

```
=IF(C8=0," ",VLOOKUP(UPPER(A8),Stock,4)*$F3*E8)
```

Cell F8 must be shown as an absolute reference for the reasons already explained. Also, as you may have noticed, the brackets have been rearranged slightly to bring the F3*E8 part of the formula inside the IF function. Without that the spreadsheet would have still multiplied the values in those cells and produced an error message whenever one of them, which means E8, was blank.

Copy all of these formulas down as far as row 14 and then try entering a few part numbers. The magic of that last trick will now be apparent.

After that all it takes is to show a few totals and the spreadsheet is complete. The formula for E16 is just:

```
=SUM(E8:E14)
```

The formula for E17 is (once the value is entered into cell F4):

```
=F4*B18
```

It should also hardly need mentioning that the formula for E18 is:

```
=SUM(F8:F14)
```

At this point, though, look at the VAT figures as they are entered into the spreadsheet in Figure 3.2. Even without a calculator it is obvious that the individual values do not add up to the total shown in E18. True, the discrepancy is slight, but it is still there nevertheless and it could cast doubt over the accuracy of the entire spreadsheet. As you may have guessed it is caused by the spreadsheet displaying only two decimal places in the relevant cells while actually working to several more and it was included here for that very reason. Such rounding errors are not vague textbook concepts, they can affect any spreadsheet at any time. That being the case, anyone feeling adventurous can try amending the formula to include the ROUND function so that it reads:

```
=IF(C8=0," ",VLOOKUP(UPPER(A8),Stock,4)*ROUND($F$3*E8,2))
```

That just leaves the Transport costs to be calculated. In this case company policy is to charge £10 for all orders less than £100, £5 for orders less than £200 and nothing for orders above that. To put that another way, welcome to the world of the nested IF function.

Where a single IF function offers two choices depending on the result of a particular test, a nested IF function can increase those choices to as many as the application calls for. That is what makes it so useful, but first the formula to be entered into cell E19 is:

```
=IF(SUM(E16:E18)<=100,10,IF(SUM(E16:E18)<=200,5,"NIL"))
```

Once again try working it through before reading the explanation. The first test is to see if the total for cells E16, E17 and E18 is less than or equal to £100. If it is, the value of £10 is returned and the formula goes no further; if not, the second action is another IF function which tests to see if the total is less than or equal to £200. Since the total must be above £100 for this second action to be involved, obviously this test is actually for totals of between £100 and £200. If this is satisfied the value £5 is returned, but if not then, as the total must be above £200, the spreadsheet will display the word 'NIL'.

All that is left now is to produce the final invoice total using the formula:

```
=SUM(E16:E19)
```

After that the cells showing this and its data label can be given a 3D effect to improve the presentation, or you may choose a different effect. These effects are available in any spreadsheet and they should be used, so experiment with a few. It can do no harm and the experience will be invaluable when designing real spreadsheets.

In spreadsheet terminology any function placed inside another function is said to be nested. While in practice any function can be nested, there is one specific instance of this where an IF function is nested inside another IF function which is known, unsurprisingly, as the nested IF function.

The technique may be simple, but it is still extremely effective with any number of potential applications. It can be extended to include as many IF functions

continued

as there are values to test for, so the possibilities are literally endless. The only point to keep in mind is that, properly speaking, the values being tested for should have been stored in separate cells which would then have been referred to in the formula. This means the values could be changed without having to edit any formulas, which makes for a more flexible spreadsheet. This flexibility was omitted here purely to keep the exercise simple.

In fact by now spreadsheets using lookup functions should present you with no problems, even if they do occasionally use large formulas. Just remember, there is nothing inherently difficult in creating these formulas and take it one step, or one function, at a time. Soon they will seem neither long nor complex.

Databases

Unfortunately not every application which calls for stored data can be created by the use of lookup functions. There will be times when only a database and its associated functions can be used.

In some ways this is complicated by the fact that there are two distinct methods of incorporating database facilities into a spreadsheet: using the built-in functions or taking the data from a separate database package. If the built-in functions are used, a database must be created in the spreadsheet itself, which is known as an internal database or an internal data source. A separate database package is obviously an external database or external data source.

To start with the external data sources it is, in fact, the work of a few mouse clicks to transfer this information into a spreadsheet.

Depending on the spreadsheet, the menu option could be something like Data; External Data; Query or Create; Database; New Query. The system may vary, but the process is identical.

Select the database or databases, choose where on the spreadsheet that data will be stored, then click the button marked 'OK'. The data will then be transferred (imported) into the spreadsheet where it can be used, manipulated or calculated as the situation calls for. The only slight problem comes from the fact that frequently not all the data stored in that database is wanted. There will be many times when only those records matching a specific criterion are needed. This criterion could be orders above a certain value, orders below a certain value, or sales of a certain product. Anything is possible, all it takes is to tell the spreadsheet what records to select (which is done after the database has been selected and before deciding where the records should be stored in a spreadsheet).

Boolean logic

This type of logic system, invented by the mathematician George Boole in 1847, breaks down any problem into a series of Yes or No answers, which is so amazingly helpful that it is now used in everything from database searches to the design of the microchip itself, with Internet searches in between.

The system works by taking two statements connected by what are known as logical operators, all of which is collectively known as the input. From this the output is calculated depending entirely on the particular logical operator used. For spreadsheets, there are three different types: AND, OR and NOT. These work as follows:

- **AND** – both conditions must be true;
- **OR** – either condition can be true;
- **NOT** – the condition is not true.

To see how this works in practice, assume the statements (inputs) are: Colour = Red and Make = Ford. Also assume that a database of cars was being searched using these two inputs plus a logical operator. The results would be as follows:

- Colour = Red **AND** Make = Ford – only red Fords would be listed.
- Colour = Red **OR** Make = Ford – red cars of any make would be listed as would all Ford cars.
- Colour = Red **NOT** Make = Ford – all red cars would be listed, with the exception of Fords.

It is by using such statements combined with logical operators that even large databases can be searched accurately. However, there is a lot more to the subject of Boolean logic, and while this brief explanation should be more than sufficient as far as spreadsheets are concerned, a word of warning should be given about an easily made mistake.

If, as an example, somebody wanted to search the above database looking for cars that were red and cars that were blue, they might enter the statement as:

Colour = Red AND Colour = Blue

If they did it would produce no matches (select no records) no matter how many red and blue cars were listed. This is because the AND operator means both statements must be true. However, if a car was red – and so matched the first statement – then by definition it could not be blue, so it would not match the second. The correct statement is:

Colour = Red OR Colour = Blue

Terminology

Once Boolean logic is understood, any records from any database can be imported into a spreadsheet for further work to be done. Since databases have their own terminology, the terms and definitions are explained in Table 3.2.

Table 3.2 Database terms and definitions

Database	A collection of records.
Record	All the information relating to a specific entry in the database. Name, address and telephone number could be the record of whoever was in the name field.
Field	A specific entry in the database. Think of a heading on a sheet of paper with a list of items underneath. The heading is the field name and the list of items underneath would be the records.
View	Sometimes the information needed is stored on more than one database. When this happens the relevant fields from the various databases are displayed together on a special form known as a View.
Query	Another special form where the fields from a database or view are shown together with any records matching the specified criteria.

The great strength of any database lies in the fact that several can be linked together and searched as one. This is known as a relational database as these linked databases will all contain related information. For example, customer names and addresses could be in one, with customer orders in another. This is done to avoid what is known as redundancy which, in this instance, means the

Making sure that the information stored in a database is correct is known as maintaining its integrity.

These relational facilities are usually claimed only by the specialised database packages which is strange because, despite what some of the handbooks might say, they are also available in spreadsheet databases. They may not be as flexible, but they can be used with very little effort.

same information being entered more than once. In the example above, if the name and address of a customer was in the same database as the details of any orders, then every time a new order was placed that same name and address would have to be entered. The relational facilities of a database do away with this by allowing the two separate files to be linked, which also has the advantage that it then becomes easy to maintain the integrity of the database. In practical terms, and still using the above example, if the customer was to change his address or telephone number, under the relational system only one entry would need to be changed. However, if that name and address appeared many times throughout a database, every occurrence would need to be changed. Not only would this be time consuming, but if even one of those entries was missed, that database would be holding incorrect information.

The only complication is that this is the one place where different spreadsheets have different ways of working. For that reason they need to be explained separately. But first, no matter which spreadsheet you are using, enter the data from Figure 3.3.

This shows the two databases which are to be linked so, once entered, name the range I10–J15 'STATION' and the range L10–N23 'RAIN'. These represent the rainfall over a certain period and the locations where it fell.

Database design

When looking at all the necessary information and trying to split it into separate databases, the first thing to decide is which of that information should only be entered once. In the above example, customer name and address should

	I	J	K	L	M	N
9	Sta	tion			Rainfall	
10	ID	Location		Date	ID	Depth
11	1	LONDON		15-Nov-99	1	2.3
12	2	MANCHESTER		15-Nov-99	2	3.1
13	3	BIRMINGHAM		16-Nov-99	3	2.7
14	4	NEWCASTLE		16-Nov-99	1	2.1
15	5	LEEDS		17-Nov-99	4	2.9
16				17-Nov-99	5	1.8
17				18-Nov-99	3	3.4
18				18-Nov-99	4	1.6
19				19-Nov-99	2	2.6
20				19-Nov-99	5	3.2
21				20-Nov-99	3	2.9
22				20-Nov-99	2	1.4
23				21-Nov-99	4	1.9
24						

Figure 3.3 The two databases to be linked

The word 'Station' was made to straddle two cells by simply entering 'Sta' into one cell and 'tion' into the next. Once the first cell was formatted for right alignment and the second for left, the two parts of the word apparently came together. In some spreadsheets an easier way would be to merge the two cells by selecting that icon from the tool bar, but this is the manual method for times when anything else might not be appropriate.

only be entered once, it being pointless to enter such information more than once, and so that can go to form a separate database. Similarly, in the rainfall spreadsheet databases, the location of the weather stations need only be entered once, especially since, in the real world, location would be considerably more than just the name of a city. (Here it was omitted to save time.) Database designers refer to this process as identifying the repeating groups.

Next, assume that a database has been created and data is being entered into it, then ask a simple question. Will the data about to be entered over-write existing data, and if so what effect will it have? If that existing data is still needed, the database needs to be redesigned. Usually this is best done by deciding which pieces of information are specifically related to each other. In the spreadsheet example, the date rain fell, the place where it fell and the amount that fell all relate to one specific rainfall incident, so they must be kept together. Everything else can go into another database, or several databases.

Even though the process is simple it is unlikely to make much sense at the moment. That will come only with practice. It also has to be said that the fairly informal method just described barely covers the subject, but it should be enough for simple spreadsheet databases. For anything more complex a dedicated database package is more likely to be the best option, along with a training course in how to use one.

The only point left to make concerns the ID numbers that were in both the spreadsheet databases just entered. These are what database designers refer to as a key field in that they are the way by which the various databases are linked. In principle, one database is searched for the value in that key field which matches a specified criterion and then that key field value is used to search another database to return whatever information was originally asked for.

To see how that works in practice, assume the spreadsheet databases above were being searched to find the area of heaviest rainfall. First the RAIN database would be searched to find the highest entry in the 'Depth' field (in this case 3.4). Then the corresponding ID number (3) would be read from the ID field, which would allow the STATION database to be searched for whichever location matched the ID number (Birmingham).

It is simple, although it does raise the final elements in database design. Firstly there must always be a key field and it must appear in more than one database. In the example above 'ID' was the key field in the STATION database and it also appeared in the RAIN database to provide the link. (It is possible for another field in the database to be the key field linking it with yet another database.)

All of this carries with it the implication that the key field must be unique. There cannot be two instances of the same key, at least not in the original database. In the STATION database each location had an ID number assigned to it which had to be unique because it referred to a specific location. However, in the RAIN database the same ID number occurred many times because it linked the event being recorded (rainfall) with the location where it happened. Think of that ID number as taking the place of the complete name and address of the location which would otherwise have had to be entered, and it should start to make sense.

Once again this is a very simplified explanation of database design, but it should be sufficient to provide the theoretical background against which databases can be created in practice. Enter the information from Figure 3.4 on the same spreadsheet as the databases. Very little of this needs to be entered straight away other than the title, the data labels in column A and D, plus the label in C13 and the location in C14. Everything else will be calculated.

	A	B	C	D	E
1			**RAINFALL SURVEY**		
2					
3	Details For:	MANCHESTER			
4				Max Rainfall	3.4
5	No. of Days	3			
6				Area	BIRMINGHAM
7	Max Depth	3.1			
8	Min Depth	1.4			
9	Avg Depth	2.37			
10					
11					
12					
13			Enter Station Name		
14			Manchester		
15					

Figure 3.4 A rainfall survey

This will search the databases previously entered and return certain, specified information. In this case entering the name of a location in C14 will return the details shown on the left of the spreadsheet, with that information on the right remaining the same. To be more exact, the information will be fixed for as long as the information in the database stays unchanged, but the principle remains the same.

Unfortunately, the one area where spreadsheets differ is in the way they handle databases. There is the Lotus way and the Excel way and they are so different that they just cannot be dealt with at the same time.

Lotus 123 databases

Before starting any database work the first thing to do is to transfer the location as entered into cell C14 into B3 so that it can act as a title for the information that will appear beneath it. Normally the way to copy the contents of one cell into another is to enter the location of the cell to be copied, which in this case would mean entering =C14 into cell B3. However, as already explained with lookup functions, there may be functions which are case sensitive and so, rather than take the risk, the best way is to enter the formula:

    @UPPER(C14)

This cell will also be used for later database searches.

First, a word about Lotus database functions. There are in fact many functions which can be used to perform various operations on databases, all of which can be easily identified as they begin with the letter D. In this way DMAX returns the largest, maximum value, DAVG the average value, and so on. Furthermore, these functions have three arguments: database, field and criteria. There is slightly more to it than that because if the criteria part of the function is omitted, the entire field of that database will be searched.

As an example, and to see this in action, in cell E6 enter the formula:

    @DMAX(RAIN,"Depth")

This looks at the RAIN database and, since no criterion was mentioned, it then searches the entire Depth field to find the maximum value there.

If the maximum rainfall for a particular location needed to be found, a criteria must be added, making the formula:

    @DMAX(RAIN,"Depth",ID=1)

Field names must always be entered between quotation marks.

This would return the maximum rainfall for the location whose ID number was 1 (London). Confusingly, although ID is itself a field name here, it is not entered between quotation marks. This because it forms part of the criteria argument where the rules are different, although why this is the case only Lotus could explain. Just accept it, enter the formula, then try experimenting by changing the ID number, perhaps even changing the function itself to something like DMIN, or DAVG.

Once you have understood all this it is time to try something a little more advanced. In cell B5 the number of days rain fell is for Manchester only and so, in plain English, the spreadsheet must first take the value in B3 and search the STATION database for the ID number associated with that location (for the ID number where the criteria is Manchester). Then it must search the RAIN database using that ID number as a criteria and count all the times the number appears. The good news is that the DCOUNT function will count all entries matching a specific criteria, but after that things start to get complicated.

To do such linked searches the function must show, in strict order:

- both database names;
- the field in the second database where the entries are to be searched for;
- the key field in each database that links them both;
- the criteria against which the first database must be searched.

So that a worked example can be shown the formula for cell B5 is in fact:

```
@DCOUNT(STATION,RAIN,"Depth",RAIN.ID=STATION.ID#AND#Location=B3)
```

As ever with long formulas they only look complicated at first. Work them through and they quickly start to make sense.

To begin with the two database names are shown, followed by the name of a field. In this case it is Depth as that is the field which will ultimately be counted to find out how many entries match the criteria. After that the spreadsheet is told that the ID field in the RAIN database matches the ID field in the STATION database (the key fields) so the databases can be linked through these. Finally the rest of the criteria are added telling the spreadsheet to start by matching whatever location name is in cell B3 with its ID number.

There is a perfectly logical sequence of events written into that formula – providing it is read backwards. Take the value stored in B3 (Manchester), look in the Location field and find the ID number that matches it, then count all records in the Depth field with a corresponding ID number. It does make sense, but there are still some points to be aware of:

- The linking (key) fields need to be entered in the format: database name, full stop, field name. For example RAIN.ID.

- The order in which those linking fields are entered is important. Reading backwards, the way the spreadsheet works, the first field should be that of the database which is searched first. In the above example the first database to be searched was STATION as that holds the ID number associated with Manchester, so the first of the linking fields to be entered had to be STATION.ID.

- The AND term is a logical operator which means that in other applications OR or NOT could just as easily be used, providing they are entered between '#' symbols.

That is a lot to take in, but like everything else it gets easier with practice. Once the principles are understood they can then be applied elsewhere with minimal effort. As proof, consider the formulas that should be entered into cells B7, B8 and B9. As these essentially look for the same information from the same set of databases it therefore follows that the formulas will be essentially the same. All that is different is the function. Enter the same formula as above, but in place of DCOUNT use DMAX, DMIN and DAVG. What could be easier or more straightforward? To prove it works, try entering the names of other locations into C14.

Finally, the formula in E8 needs to be considered, which was included to show how the same procedure can also work in reverse. Instead of taking a location and returning a value, this takes a value and returns a location. Other than that the procedure is identical – try to work out what the formula should be before reading any further. Just remember that the formula should return the location associated with the value (rainfall) currently being shown in cell E6, which means that the function to be used is DGET.

Purely by way of confirmation the formula is:

```
@DGET(STATION,RAIN,"Location",STATION.ID=RAIN.ID#AND#Depth=E6)
```

Microsoft Excel databases

Depending entirely on your point of view, database creation in Excel is either more primitive or simpler than in Lotus. It is certainly different, to the point where an extra section has to be added to the spreadsheet. Therefore, start by adding the information in Figure 3.5. For the time being only the data labels in row 2 need be entered; the rest will be done later.

	I	J	K	L	M	N
1						
2	ID	Location		Date	ID	Depth
3	3	MANCHESTER			2	3.4
4						

Figure 3.5 Database creation in Excel

The first thing to do is to transfer the location as entered into cell C14 into B3 so that it can act as a title for the information that will appear beneath it. This cell will also be used for later database searches, but first some theory.

In order for the database functions to work in Excel they need three pieces of information – three arguments – which are:

- database
- field
- criteria.

The first of these is obvious (a spreadsheet must be told what database to search), as is the second (a spreadsheet must also be told what field to look in). At first the third might also seem obvious, since a spreadsheet must also be told what to search the database for, but that still leaves the question of exactly how that criteria is entered into the function.

There are two possible ways of doing it:

Remember, the best way to copy the contents of one cell into another is to enter the cell reference.

- If every record in a field must be included, the criteria is the range of cells corresponding to that field.
- If only those records which match a more specific criteria are to be considered, the criteria is just two cell references which are entered in the section of the spreadsheet just created.

To see how the first method works in practice, in cell E4 enter the formula:

```
=DMAX(RAIN,"Depth",N10:N23)
```

This function searches for a maximum value that meets certain conditions being defined by the arguments of the function. In this case those conditions are the name of the database (RAIN), the field within that database which is to be searched (which must be entered within quotation marks) and any supplementary criteria. Here there is none, so the formula is completed by showing the cell range for the entire field. Had there been a need to refine the search further, such as, for example, finding the maximum depth of rainfall that fell in a particular location, a different criteria would have been entered.

Cell B5 shows the number of days that rain fell in Manchester. To do that the spreadsheet must take the location as shown in cell B3, search the STATION database to find the ID number associated with that location, and count all the times rainfall was recorded against that location ID in the RAIN database. In Excel this must be done in two stages.

First, in cell J3 enter the formula:

```
=UPPER(C14)
```

As we know, this simply takes the location name as entered into C14 and converts it into upper case so that it can be used to search the database. This is the key to using databases in Excel. That section of spreadsheet which had to be created specifically is in fact the criteria area. Anything entered there becomes the criteria for database searches. To see how that works in practice, in cell M3 enter the formula:

```
=DGET(STATION,"ID",J2:J3)
```

The function DGET returns one specific value according to a specific set of conditions which are defined by its arguments. The first two (STATION and ID) are self-explanatory, being the database and field names. The third is much more specific. Cell J2 holds the name of a field within the STATION database, in this case 'Location', and cell J3 holds the name of a particular location. In more technical terms, J3 holds a value of the Location field. Putting all this together means that the spreadsheet will search the Location field of the STATION database until it finds an entry which matches that shown in cell J3, at which point it will return the ID number associated with that entry.

To extend the theory side of things, those two cell references (J2 and J3) form the criteria as they tell the spreadsheet what field to search and what value to search that field for. In this case it was an ID number, but it could have been anything else. For example, if the value 2.1 was entered into cell N3, the criteria N2:N3 would search the depth field for that value and return either the Location ID or the date, depending on the rest of the formula. The value could even be entered as >2.1 and the spreadsheet would then search for values greater than 2.1.

The slight problem here is with the DGET function. This returns a specific value, which means if two or more values match the criteria, an error message will be displayed.

It is also possible to search the database using more than one condition just by adding those conditions in the criteria range of the spreadsheet. For example, to find the average depth of rainfall in both Leeds and Manchester, enter the relevant ID for Leeds in cell M3 and that for Manchester in M4. After that use the DAVG function with a criteria range of M2:M4.

Similarly, to find the number of days that rainfall in Manchester exceeded, say, 2.0 inches, enter the ID for Manchester in cell M3 and the value >2.0 in cell N3. The function DCOUNT will then do the rest – once the criteria range has been entered as M2:N3.

To search a database for one condition or another (ie using the Boolean logical operator 'OR') just enter the criteria on different rows. For example, to find the number of days that rain fell in London OR that rain fell on a specific date, enter the date in cell L3 and the ID for London in cell M4.

It is also possible to enter a calculation into the criteria range and use that as the basis for a database search which explains the formula entered in cell M3. Since this returns the ID number associated with whatever Station name was entered into C14, and since this value is in the criteria area of the spreadsheet, it can then be used for further searches.

To see how that works, in cell B5 enter the formula:

```
=DCOUNT(RAIN,"Depth",M2:M3)
```

This should need no explanation, nor should there be any need to explain how the various formulas fit together to return what a simple inspection of the database will show to be the right result. In much the same way it should be obvious that the formulas for cells B7, B8 and B9 are identical apart from the fact that they use the functions DMAX, DMIN and DAVG respectively. Those who enjoy the magic of spreadsheets might try entering a different station name into cell C14 just to see the figures change, but, other than that, everything should be straightforward.

In fact, there is only one more formula to be entered in the entire spreadsheet which is there purely to show the system in reverse. So far a Station name has been used to return a value; now a value will be used to return a Station name – in this case the station which recorded the highest level of rainfall as already shown in cell E4.

First enter the criteria in the criteria area, which is no more difficult than, in cell N3, showing the cell reference:

```
=E4
```

This transfers the value in cell E4 so it can then be used as the criteria in the formula which is to be entered into cell I3. Once again this is another formula designed to return a value into the criteria range so that it can then be used as the basis for another database search. In this case, of course, it must return the station ID associated with the depth as shown in cell N3, which makes the formula:

```
=DGET(RAIN,"ID",N2:N3)
```

It should also go without saying that this ID number can then be used in a further search to return the Station name, in which case the formula to be entered into cell E6 is:

```
=DGET(STATION,"Location",I2:I3)
```

If further entries are made to any database its range name will have to be redefined to include the extra cells.

This technique can be applied to more than just databases. Any lookup table or list can be made easier to use in the same way, so it is a trick worth keeping in mind.

There are two other points which should be mentioned about using databases in Excel. The first is that when designing spreadsheets the criteria range can be placed anywhere, although it is best not to put it underneath the database itself. That way further entries can be made to the database without the risk of encroaching on the criteria area because if the criteria area had to be moved, all the cell references in all the formulas would have to be changed.

Secondly, a problem with searching any list is that the entries in that list must be known. Imagine trying to enter a city name in the above example without knowing which cities were included in the rainfall survey, or in the database, which comes to the same thing. In lists or databases far longer than the above example this would be an issue which could seriously affect people's ability to use the spreadsheet. The solution in this case is a drop-down list.

With the cursor on the input cell (C14), select 'Data Validation' from the Tools menu. Then, in the box that appears, click on 'Allow' and from the available choices select 'List'. You will have to enter the range of cells holding that list (J11–J15 in this example), then click on 'OK'. Cell C14 will now have a small arrow by the side of it which, if you click on it, will display a list of all the cities in the database. You can select any of them clicking on it.

Data sources

One question likely to spring to mind is when should a lookup table be used in preference to a database, or vice versa. In general terms this is an answer that will arise naturally as the spreadsheet is being designed. Once it has been decided what the spreadsheet should do, determining how it should be done will point the way to the right function which will, in turn, make the decision automatic.

Whether the data source should be internal or external (built into the spread-sheet or taken from an outside database package) in many ways depends on the application. If the data already exists in an external database, it obviously makes sense to use the data filter option and import the data needed into the spreadsheet. However, if this is a new application where the data has yet to be entered, using the spreadsheet database functions will be both quicker and easier (if only because no one will need to learn how to use a database package).

There will perhaps come a time when too many records, or a too complex data-base structure, will force the issue and make the use of a database package the only viable option, but that is something that can only be decided on an indi-vidual basis. Until then, for the sake of simplicity, stick to using spreadsheets.

Charts   4

There is more to creating graphs than selecting the Chart option from the menu. In fact, knowing which graph to use under which circumstances is a skill in itself, particularly with the number of graphs on offer.

Let us begin with an explanation of what the various types of graph actually do, starting with the easiest.

Line	A line graph shows trends and for this reason is often used to display a single set of figures which change over time. Alternatively, more than one line could be drawn as a simple way of comparing one set of values against another.
Bar	This is used to show pieces of information which are related but are not dependent on each other. An example here could be the total sales of individual sales staff.
Stacked bar	Here the height of the bar is made up of different segments representing sub-totals. For example, it could represent not just the total sales of each member of a sales team but also sales of individual products.
Pie	This shows different values expressed as a percentage of the whole; for example, each individual product as a percentage of the total sales achieved.

Let's create a few of those graphs. Start by entering the information from Figure 4.1. There are no hidden formulas to be entered, other than the totals – this is just a simple base set of figures.

	A	B	C	D	E	F	G
1	Product	France	Germany	Spain	Italy	Britain	Total
2	AAA	23	35	14	17	21	110
3	BBB	42	19	27	14	19	121
4	CCC	6	4	2	5	2	19
5	DDD	9	7	6	8	3	33
6							
7	Total	80	65	49	44	45	283
8							

Figure 4.1 A simple base set of figures

Creating a chart

Creating a chart is easy. Click on the Chart icon at the top of the screen and answer the questions in the dialog boxes that appear automatically.

The first, and most obvious, question is which figures will be used to create the chart and where on the spreadsheet they can be found. In other words, which range of cells is the spreadsheet to work with.

In Excel the first question is actually what type of chart you want, but as deciding what to chart is a slightly more logical way of doing things, it will be explained this way round.

In spreadsheet jargon a list of figures which will form a single entry in a chart is known as a data series.

In Lotus 123 a bar chart will appear at first: if a different type is required, select Chart Properties from the menu or right-click on the chart area.

Here an easy mistake to make is to select too many cells and so make the chart unnecessarily complicated. For example, in Figure 4.1 the range should be A1 to F5, which includes the data labels but excludes the totals. Doing this means the chart will show just the product and country information, which is all that is needed. Not only are the totals unnecessary, but showing them would force the spreadsheet to calculate the scale of that graph based on those high total figures, making the much smaller individual figures harder to read.

There will also be times when not every figure in that data range will need to be charted. For example, in the above spreadsheet a chart to show the sales of just one product compared to the total sales of all products may be needed. How can those particular values be chosen when there are other cells in between them? Here the easiest way is to copy the relevant cells, including the appropriate data labels, to a different part of the spreadsheet where they can be side by side and then use that as the data series for creating the chart.

Of course, once the figures to be charted have been chosen, the remaining question is what type of chart will be created.

To begin with in this example use a simple bar chart, select an area of the spreadsheet where the chart is to be displayed, and let the process begin. In the Excel chart wizard there are other steps to follow, but in this case click on 'Finish' just to see the end result.

It will be immediately obvious that this shows the sales of each product grouped according to country, but what happens if you want something different? Suppose the idea was to show the sales for each country grouped by product.

This is another area where the spreadsheets differ in operation. In Excel the same dialog box that asks for the data range also includes two more options: Series in Rows and Series in Columns. In this case choosing Series in Rows would group the information according to country, while with Series in Columns the grouping would be by product. There is also a preview of what the chart would look like.

In Lotus 123 first select Chart Properties, then Ranges, then Options. Once again there will be the same two choices of series by row or column and there is also a diagram to explain the differences between the two.

Now you have created your chart, you can concentrate on titles. No matter what the spreadsheet, right-click over the chart area and select Properties. The titles can then be added from the dialog boxes that will appear.

Now would be a good time to create a few charts. For the moment stick to line, bar and pie charts, but using Figure 4.1 as a basis, try experimenting with the options. See what the various 3D effects look like, try changing the typeface or size of the titles, or try any other change the spreadsheet will allow.

Now you can consider some of the more specialised forms of chart, starting with the easiest: the histogram.

In Excel, if a new chart is being created the dialog boxes will appear just by completing all the steps in the chart wizard.

Histograms

A histogram is no more than a bar chart with what is known as a continuous variable along the X axis. To put that in less jargon-laden terms, where the horizontal or X axis on a bar chart could be the names of anything, such as products, countries or even sales people, in a histogram it will be a range of numbers. Typically this is then used to show the frequency with which each number occurred.

For example, the horizontal (X) axis could show a range of temperatures with the first point being 0–10 degrees, the second 11–20, and so on. The range itself can be any set of values, but they must be continuous, which means each value must lead on to the next. There must be no gaps in the range. Assuming, for the sake of example, that these points along the graph showed a range of temperatures, the completed histogram could show, say, five readings in the 0–10 range, seven in the 11–20 range, and so on. (These readings, or frequencies to give them their correct name, will be shown as bars on the chart.)

Histograms can, therefore, be extremely useful. However, while they can be created easily, they cannot be created automatically. Not one single spreadsheet package can create histograms at the touch of a button; some work first has to be done.

To begin with, the frequencies have to be calculated as this is what the spreadsheet will eventually plot onto a graph. This might already be done depending on the source of the data, for example the data might come from a questionnaire, so all it would take would be to count the number of ticks in a box. However, on the assumption that the data in its raw form already exists on the spreadsheet, something else is needed. This will be illustrated here using an example.

Figure 4.2 shows temperature readings taken over a 12-day period. These can be entered exactly as they appear. The next part needs more of an explanation.

	A	B	C	D	E
1	DAY	TEMP			
2	1	12			
3	2	23		BIN	FREQUENCY
4	3	15		15	4
5	4	11		20	2
6	5	26		25	3
7	6	19		30	1
8	7	24		35	2
9	8	32			0
10	9	24			
11	10	15			
12	11	35			
13	12	17			
14					

Figure 4.2 Temperature readings taken over 12 days

Before a spreadsheet can decide whether a number falls between a certain range of values it has to know what that range of values is. In spreadsheet terms these are known as bins. Think of them as pigeonholes – the spreadsheet then works its way down a list of numbers and puts each one into the appropriate pigeonhole. After that all it has to do is count how many numbers are in each pigeonhole.

In Figure 4.2 the range of values, or bins, as shown in cells D4 to D8 are: 0–15, 16–20, 21–25, 26–30, 30–35. This is slightly confusing because in any spreadsheet only the top value is shown. The spreadsheet itself does the rest. Again these have to be entered by hand – there is no formula involved, but once they are entered the frequency can be calculated.

In Lotus 123 this is done from the menu. Select Range, Analyse, Distribution and for the range of values to count enter the cell range B2:B13. For the bin range enter D4:D8 and the relevant frequency figures will appear in the column to the right.

In Excel things are a bit more complicated. Here a special function known as FREQUENCY is needed. This is known as an array function. This means any calculations are performed on a range, or array, of figures rather than just the value stored in a single cell. It also means the function has to be entered in a special way, but first the arguments of the FREQUENCY function are: data_array and bins_array. The data_array argument is the figures which the spreadsheet will work through to calculate their frequency (B2:B13 in this case), while bins_array is the range of values it must sort the figures into (D4:D8 in the example).

To enter it, highlight the cell range E4 to E9 as this is the area over which the figures will be shown. Then, without pressing the Enter key or the OK button, type in the following:

```
=FREQUENCY(B2:B13,D4:D8)
```

The spreadsheet must be told this is an array function: press CTRL plus Shift plus Enter simultaneously. When this is done the values will appear as shown.

Even if it was not obvious before, anyone can now see that there are 4 temperature readings in the range 0–15 degrees, 2 in the range 16–20 and so on. In other words, the frequency of those temperature readings has been assigned to those value ranges.

This still leaves at least one unresolved issue: why, no matter what the spreadsheet, is there always one more frequency figure than there are bin ranges? This is what might be described as an overflow bin. If any figures in the data range (B2:B13 in the example) are higher than the maximum value in the bin range (D4:D8), they will be shown here. This is not only a safety device to prevent a few atypical values from generating error messages, it also means that, if necessary, only a certain range of values can be considered from the data as a whole. For example, the bins in the above spreadsheet could have been set as, say, 10–11, 11–12, and so on up to 20, so that any values beyond that would be put into the overflow bin where they could be ignored when the histogram came to be created.

The creation of a histogram is slightly complicated by two factors:

- Spreadsheets think of figures as values to be plotted on a graph, leaving the data labels to be drawn from those cells containing text. However, in this case the figures in the bin range need to be shown as labels along the horizontal axis of the graph and not as figures on it.

- Even if these bin values were converted into text, they would still only show a single figure and not the range of figures they actually represent. In the example above, a bin value may be shown as 20, but it represents all temperature readings in the range of 16–20; it is that which should be shown as the data label on the histogram.

It is, therefore, time to use another function which, with a little bit of coaxing, will not only convert the bin values into text but will also allow the full range of those values to be shown. The function in question is CONCATENATE.

According to the dictionary, concatenate means a series or combination.

For those using the Paste Function icon in Excel and entering the figures in the dialog box that it brings up, there is no need to enter the hyphen between quotation marks. Excel does that automatically. For those using Lotus 123 there is no direct equivalent.

Concatenate

To see this in action choose another cell, say D14, and in that enter:

`=CONCATENATE(0,"-",D4)`

Once this is done the cell will actually display 0–15 which is, of course, the range of temperature readings that the bin value in cell D4 refers to. After that the other bin values need to be considered and converted. This is slightly more complicated in that the range of each bin value starts from one more than the preceding value and stops at the value shown. If the value in a cell is 20 and the preceding value is 15 then the range of values is in fact 16–20.

Taking this into account means that the formula in cell D15 should be:

`=CONCATENATE(D4+1,"-",D5)`

The result will show 16–20. If this formula is then copied down as far as cell D18, all the value ranges will be shown. Then, in cell E14, enter the very simple formula:

`=E4`

Copying this down to cell E18 will put a copy of the frequency results next to their associated bin ranges. Now creating a simple bar chart using the range D14:E18 is all that it takes to produce a histogram.

XY graph

Generally referred to as a scatter graph or XY scatter graph, this shows the relationship of one figure to another and can also plot a trend line through the data, assuming there is a trend to be plotted. One of the strengths of the XY graph is that it can analyse large amounts of data to see if there are trends hidden within it.

Enter the data from Figure 4.3 (on page 86). Assume this to be a report from a call centre which provides a help desk for two products: AAA and BBB. The report is informative as far as it goes, except that it fails to answer the questions that would make it a valuable management reporting tool. Are the calls for either product increasing or decreasing? If one is increasing and the other decreasing, by how much, if at all, does the one compensate for the other? What general decisions could be taken based on these figures?

Here a simple line graph would be inconclusive, whether it was based on one product, both products or the total calls received each day. (Try it and see.) Similarly, the moving average figures provide no real help either, for product BBB especially. That one single high figure shown in cell F5 is enough to distort all the preceding results. In short, the data are too erratic to be meaningful without further analysis of the kind provided by an XY graph.

Although the moving average figures have nothing to do with XY graphs, they are shown for one reason. Being able to calculate moving averages is such a useful skill, which can be applied to so many spreadsheets, that everyone should know how to do it, especially as it is so easy.

The spreadsheet was made slightly easier to follow simply by reducing the width of columns B, E and H and then changing the background colour.

The formula in D5 is simply:

```
=AVERAGE(C$4:C5)
```

Initially this calculates the average for just the two cells (C4 and C5), but when this formula is copied down the column the absolute reference anchors the first

Date	AAA	Avg.	BBB	Avg.	Total
CALL CENTRE - REPORT					
PRODUCT					
15/11/1999	23		32		55
16/11/1999	15	19.00	43	37.50	58
17/11/1999	26	21.33	28	34.33	54
18/11/1999	17	20.25	31	33.50	48
19/11/1999	31	22.40	29	32.60	60
20/11/1999	14	21.00	29	32.00	43
21/11/1999	24	21.43	39	33.00	63
22/11/1999	21	21.38	23	31.75	44
23/11/1999	12	20.33	26	31.11	38
24/11/1999	18	20.10	35	31.50	53
25/11/1999	15	19.64	32	31.55	47
26/11/1999	28	20.33	34	31.75	62
27/11/1999	36	21.54	36	32.08	72
28/11/1999	17	21.21	32	32.07	49
29/11/1999	23	21.33	31	32.00	54
30/11/1999	31	21.94	30	31.88	61
01/12/1999	26	22.18	33	31.94	59
02/12/1999	23	22.22	26	31.61	49

Figure 4.3 A call centre report

cell reference in place and extends the number of cells over which the average is to be calculated. Try it and see the effect. Then do the same for product BBB. Finally, just to complete the spreadsheet, show the total figures. As only two cells are involved the SUM function would be unnecessarily complicated. A far easier method would be to enter into cell I4 the formula:

    =C4+F4

Copying that down the column will then complete the spreadsheet, at which point it is time to create the graph.

Creating an XY graph

When creating an XY graph the first point to be decided is which is the independent variable to be shown on the X axis and which is the Y axis dependent variable.

The next point to keep in mind is that whatever range of values is used for the X axis, it must be sorted into ascending order. There is nothing difficult about sorting a range of values in a spreadsheet. The only point is that all the cells associated with those values must be sorted at the same time. For example, assume that a spreadsheet held two columns of cells whose values were as shown below:

Smithson	23
Smith	34
Jones	45

The independent variable is the one that is measured along the bottom of the graph. In this case this is obviously the date, as one day will follow the next no matter how many calls were received. In much the same way, anything that is not dependent on the figures being entered is by definition independent and so belongs along the X axis. Just remember that the whole point of an XY graph is to show how one measurement varies against another. The measurement that varies forms the Y, or vertical, axis.

In computer terms, alphabetical order and ascending order mean the same thing.

In Excel you can sort the names column from the Data menu; in Lotus this is done from the Range menu.

If that first column of names was then sorted into alphabetical order, only the order of those names would change. The values alongside them would remain as they were so that, in this case, Jones would have a value of 23 and Smithson a value of 45. Given that these values could be sales made or products bought, they should obviously remain associated with the right name. So simply highlight both columns and then sort the names column.

This time the values will stay associated with the right name.

It is possible to sort on more than one value. For example, assume a spreadsheet had the values in three columns as shown below:

Smith	John	23
Smith	Fred	45
Jones	Alan	56

If the columns were sorted on surnames only then Smith John would still be ahead of Smith Fred which is obviously wrong. Therefore a secondary sort should be done on the column storing the first names to correct this. Once again this is easy because when the Sort option is chosen from the menu, the facility is included to sort on more than one cell range.

Once the values are in the right order it is time to create the XY graph. To begin, the relevant cells that will be used must be copied to somewhere else on the spreadsheet. While these could be copied in any order, most spreadsheets assume that the leftmost column in the range is the X axis and so it makes sense to start with whatever will form that X axis and then put the other values to the right of that. Therefore copy the dates in cells A4 to A21 to, say, K4 to K21 (in this case there is no need to convert them into text format) and then copy the Total figures in cells I4 to I21 into L4 to L21.

Next create a chart as usual and select the XY or Scatter option to produce a graph that will, eventually, look like the one in Figure 4.4.

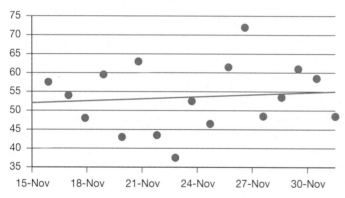

Figure 4.4 XY graph with trend line

Ignoring the trend line, which will be added later, look to see if any patterns are immediately obvious. For example, there could be higher than normal levels of demand occurring at regular intervals along the graph which might repay further analysis. In the call centre example this could be something like a lot of calls being received every Monday morning, which might suggest cus-

If the Chart menu is not already on the menu bar at the top of the screen, click somewhere in the chart area and it will appear.

tomers were having problems over the weekend and so would point the way towards longer opening hours for that call centre. (This is not shown in the spreadsheet because such trends only become apparent with far more data than could be practically entered in an example like this.)

The trend line

Next, the trend line has to be created. Select the Chart menu, then choose Add Trend Line in Excel or Series, Series Trend in Lotus.

Choose Linear from the list of options and the line will be added automatically. After that comes the question of what it actually means.

In simple terms, the spreadsheet attempts to plot what is known as a line of best fit between all the points. What this means is that the line will not necessarily come on or near any of the points, but will instead come as close as it can to as many points as it can without deviating from that straight line. The mathematical technique for doing this is known as regression analysis and will be explained further in Chapter 6. Furthermore, as the example shows, it has the added advantage of discounting any abnormally high or low figures to produce a result which is more representative of the data as a whole.

In the example it can be seen that there is a slight upward trend to the number of calls received which was not immediately apparent even on the small number of figures that were used to produce the graph. Had there been hundreds, or even thousands, of figures to work through, no one could have spotted the trend, especially as it was formed out of what were essentially random figures. If necessary, a similar graph could be produced for each individual product. It is even possible to show both products and the total on the same graph (look for Add Data Series on the menu), but that could lead to a confusing number of lines and points, so do it with care.

Nevertheless, even on such a simple example as this the value of an XY graph can be seen, both as a way of presenting data and as a way of performing a first-stage analysis on that data.

Area graph

This can best be described as a combination of line graph and stacked bar graph. It is used when a trend needs to be shown, but that trend is a combination of more than one item. For example, if there was a rising, or falling, trend in total sales but that total was made up of several products, an area graph could show how each product contributed to the trend.

When creating area graphs it is best to show the figures (the data series) with the least variation on the bottom of the graph, with the figures above it arranged in order of variation. There is no technical reason for doing this; it just looks better.

Hi-lo graph

Also known as a stock graph, this is used to show not just the maximum and minimum values for any set of readings, such as temperature or stock prices, but also the difference between them. For any point along the X axis three values are needed, known as the high, low and closing (in Lotus 123 just the high and low are needed). The chart will then display those points with a vertical line connecting them so that their volatility or the amount of change can be seen at a glance.

Radar graph

This is used when items need to be compared using a variety of criteria. For example, if two products were being evaluated, their test scores might be as follows:

TEST	A	B	C	D	E	F
Product 1	23	34	45	55	64	72
Product 2	76	66	54	46	32	21

When plotted on a radar graph, this would give the result shown in Figure 4.5.

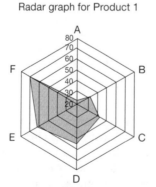
Radar graph for Product 1

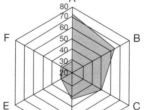
Radar graph for Product 2

Figure 4.5 Two typical radar graphs

We can see that one product overwhelmingly favours one set of test conditions while with the other the opposite is true.

Radar graphs can be useful in this way, but to be worthwhile they need several comparison figures. Five should be considered the minimum.

The above graphs are likely to be suitable for most applications. However, there will be times when something else is needed, so the next step is to consider other graphs which can be created out of the standard types. Of these, perhaps the most useful is the Z graph.

Z graph

This takes its name from the fact that it uses three lines which, when the chart is completed, form the letter Z. These three lines are:

- a base line;
- a total or maximum line;
- a cumulative line which connects the other two together.

This might make it seem like a strange sort of graph, but when it comes to plotting any series of figures which have a cumulative value, a Z graph can highlight a situation few other graphs can even show.

To see how this works, and how to create one, start by entering the information shown in Figure 4.6.

This is just a standard budget versus actual report of the kind created by every organisation in the world. There is nothing particularly special about it, nor about the way it was created, but it is still worth a second look.

	A	B	C	D	E	F	G	H	I	J	K	L	M	N
1		Jan	Feb	Mar	Apr	May	Jun	Jul	Aug	Sep	Oct	Nov	Dec	Total
2														
3	Budget	21	19	23	19	22	23	21	22	23	22	23	22	260
4	Cumulative	21	40	63	82	104	127	148	170	193	215	238	260	
6	Actual	24	24	27	25	26	28	24	27					205
7	Cumulative	24	48	75	100	126	154	178	205					
9	Variance	3	5	4	6	4	5	3	5	-23	-22	-23	-22	-55
10	Cumulative	3	8	12	18	22	27	30	35	12	-10	-33	-55	
11														
12	Projected	24	48	75	100	126	154	178	205	228	250	273	295	
13														

Figure 4.6 A budget versus actual report

Firstly, the figures were split into easier-to-read sections just by adding some shading around those sections, an effect that was enhanced by reducing the height of the rows of cells in between them. This is simple and should always be done. Far too many spreadsheets are presented as huge blocks of figures when with only a little more effort they could be turned into something readable and more easily understandable.

Next, the figures themselves. Obviously, the budget figures have to be entered by hand, as do the actuals, but everything else can be calculated. In this way the cumulative budget figure shown in cell C4 is calculated by the formula:

```
=B4+C3
```

This, and the fact that it needs to be copied along the row, should need no further explanation. Instead, think about the cumulative actual figure shown in C7. This only needs to calculate a figure if there is an entry in the cell above it, C6, otherwise it should remain blank. While this formula could be entered each month when the actuals for that month were also entered, on the basis that any work on a spreadsheet should be done when it is being created and not when it is being used, the formula is:

```
=IF(C6=0," ",C6+B7)
```

Once again this repeats the trick used earlier of keeping a cell blank until a figure needs to be shown.

The variance cumulative figure in C10 is, once again, easily calculated by the formula:

```
=C9+B10
```

This just leaves the projected figure in C12 to be calculated. Here the formula must calculate the total for the previous projected figure plus the actual unless no actual figure exists for that month, in which case it must take the budget figure. In other words, it must test the cell holding the actual figure and if there is an entry it must use that in the calculation; if not, it must use the budget figure, which means that the formula is:

```
=IF(C6=0,C3+B12,C6+B12)
```

Studying the spreadsheet should make the formula obvious. Then, once the relevant totals have been added, the spreadsheet is ready for use. The Z graph can be created.

Start by copying the relevant cells to somewhere else on the spreadsheet so that they look like Table 4.1.

Table 4.1 The relevant cells to be copied

	Jan	Feb	Mar	Apr	May	Jun	Jul	Aug	Sep	Oct	Nov	Dec
Total	260	260	260	260	260	260	260	260	260	260	260	260
Budget	21	19	23	19	22	23	21	22	23	22	23	22
Projected	24	48	75	100	126	154	178	205	228	250	273	295
Actual	24	48	75	100	126	154	178	205				

For reasons that will be made clear later, the actual figures must be copied last. Also, when the cell reference for the total figure is entered, remember to use absolute cell addressing ($N$3) so it can be safely copied along the row.

After that create a line chart using this cell range and the finished result will, eventually, look like Figure 4.7.

If nothing else, this shows how the Z graph got its name. The projected line was changed to the same colour as the actual and was also changed to a dotted or broken line. In this way, as the two are identical, where an actual figure exists, it was made to appear as one continuous line but with the forecasted element shown in the conventional manner (dotted). This was why the actual figures had to be the last entered into the cell range before the chart was created – anywhere else and the actual line would have been shown dropping to

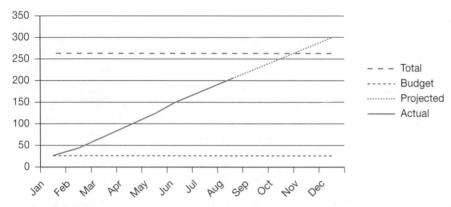

Figure 4.7 A Z graph

zero in the months where no actual figures were entered. However, due to a quirk in the way spreadsheets operate, by entering these figures last the empty cells were ignored.

So, Z graphs are useful when there is a total or maximum figure to be taken into account. Here it was the annual budget figure, but it could just as easily have been something else, such as sales for the previous year so performance in the current year could be judged. The diagonal bar being a mixture of actual and budget shows the likelihood of the total being achieved or exceeded and also when that will happen. With the bottom line showing what is expected to happen on a month-by-month basis, a great deal of information is packed into a clearly visible display.

Log graph

One of the problems of using graphs is that they can sometimes give a false impression of the way figures are changing. For example, if a graph had a scale where one inch represented 100 units, an increase of 100 to 200 would be represented by exactly the same slope as an increase of 1100 to 1200, despite the fact that in one case the actual increase is 100% and in the other a mere 10%. Since this can create a false understanding of the figures, where the rate of change is needed a log graph should be used. For example, consider Table 4.2.

Table 4.2 A period where prices are rising by 20% a year

Period	Price	Log of Price	Difference of Logs
1	100	2.000000	
2	120	2.0792	0.0792
3	144	2.1584	0.0792
4	172	2.2375	0.0792
5	206	2.3167	0.0792

This shows a period where prices are rising by a highly inflationary 20% per year. However, if the price was plotted, the graph would show an ever steepening line, while if the difference between the log of those prices was plotted, it would show a horizontal line because the rate of change remained constant.

It therefore follows that where the rate of change is to be shown, the values concerned should be converted into their log and the difference between those logs should be plotted; something that can be done easily by using the function LOG.

Creating graphs is easy, but sometimes graphs can confuse more than they clarify. For that reason always keep in mind the golden rule: when designing a graph, think not of what information should be included but what information is to be extracted from it. If you do that, you won't make too many mistakes.

What if 5

In a real-world spreadsheet, these tools could be combined in any way or even used in any combination with any other function, such is the flexibility of a spreadsheet.

It can also take a row of input values and a column of formulas, but for the time being let's stick with the explanation given here. That way everything is kept as simple as possible until you understand the process.

'What if' describes the subject exactly because that is what it is all about: taking a set of figures and asking: What if they were to change? This chapter will concern itself with the three ways this can be done:

■ data tables,

■ scenario managers

■ goal seeking.

Although they are all valuable tools for the analysis of data, they are each sufficiently different to mean that, here at least, they must be treated separately.

Data tables

A row of formulas and a column of input values is first taken. Every formula is calculated against every input value to produce a series of figures known as a data table.

While data tables are essentially simple in operation, they come with their own terminology which should be learned and understood.

Data table	The range of cells where the results of all the calculations are stored.
Input values	A series of figures which will be used by each formula in turn to produce the data table.
Input cell	A single blank cell which the spreadsheet uses to store the result of each calculation before transferring that result to the data table. The input cell is then used to store the result of the next calculation, and so on.

To see how all of this works, and to start creating a data table, consider the spreadsheet in Figure 5.1. This takes specified sums of money in pounds sterling and converts them into US dollars at a variety of exchange rates. Start with the formula in cell C8 which in its simplest form is:

=B8*5000

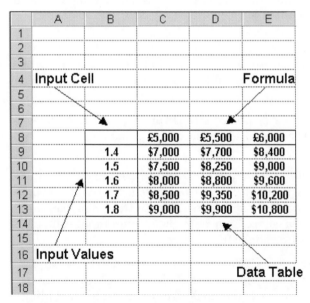

Figure 5.1 Converting pounds into dollars

This illustrates the first principle of creating data tables: every formula must refer to the input cell. Even though it is blank, and must always be blank, nevertheless the part of the formula that uses the input values must always refer to the input cell, not the cells where the input values are stored.

The only slight problem with doing this is that as the input cell is blank, the formula as it stands multiplies 5000 by zero to give the result, zero. To prevent that happening the formula should be:

```
=IF(B8=0,5000,B8*5000)
```

While this does not affect any subsequent calculations, the figure on which those calculations are based will appear on the spreadsheet to make it easier to read.

After this, once similar formulas are entered into D8 and E8, the data table can be created. The method varies between spreadsheet programs.

For Excel	Highlight the entire range of cells, including the input values and formulas, which in this case is B8 to E13. From the menu select Data and then Table. In the dialog box that appears enter a cell reference for the column input cell only, which here is B8. Click OK.
For Lotus	From the menu select Range, Analyse, What-If Table. In the dialog box that appears enter the cell reference for the input cell, B8 in this case, then the entire range of cells including the input values and formulas, which in this case is B8 to E13. Click OK.

In both cases the data table will then be calculated.

While this demonstrates how easy it is to create a data table, it does nothing to explain why or when a data table should be used. For that a different spreadsheet is required, so start by entering the information from Figure 5.2.

	A	B	C	D	E
17					
18			DISCOUNT		
19		Unit Cost	1000	5000	10000
20	Part A	2.75	1	0.975	0.95
21	Part B	4.5	1	0.98	0.925
22	Part C	8.9	1	1	0.96
23	Part D	6.25	1	0.95	0.9
24					

Figure 5.2 The DISCOUNT lookup table

There are no formulas involved here. This is just a simple lookup table which should be given the name DISCOUNT, although remember that the range to be named is A19 to E23. The title above it is there for guidance only.

Then enter the main part of the spreadsheet, as in Figure 5.3.

This is a very stripped-down version of a spreadsheet, so stripped in fact that most of the design rules have been ignored to leave the data table by itself.

This assumes that a product is made up of four components. The value of these components is shown in the lookup table together with the various quantity discounts on offer for each of those components.

The lookup table holds the value by which the unit cost should be multiplied to obtain the actual cost including discount. This was done this way for the sake of simplicity, and should not normally be the case.

	A	B	C	D
1				
2		1000	5000	10000
3		#N/A	#N/A	#N/A
4	Part A	£2.75	£2.68	£2.61
5	Part B	£4.50	£4.41	£4.16
6	Part C	£8.90	£8.90	£8.54
7	Part D	£6.25	£5.94	£5.63
8				
9	Labour	£12.65	£12.65	£12.65
10				
11	Total Cost	£35.05	£34.58	£33.59
12				

Figure 5.3 A stripped-down version of a spreadsheet

The discounts for each component are different in every case, which raises the interesting question: What will the cost of the finished product be for various levels of manufacture? This is something the data table can calculate easily.

Once the data labels in column A are entered, the rest can be done with the right formula. This, as should be obvious, looks up the unit cost of each component and then multiplies it by the appropriate discount factor. In this case, of course, the value would be something like 'Part A' which should be entered into cell A3. Then the formula can be created. Here this is slightly complicated by the fact that the lookup table must be referred to twice so the two values returned can then be multiplied together. While this is far from complicated, it does make for a fairly long formula, but one that nobody should have any trouble either creating or understanding. It is:

```
=VLOOKUP(A3,DISCOUNT,2)*VLOOKUP(A3,DISCOUNT,3)
```

Depending on the spreadsheet, the column offset number in each function may need to be altered. (See Chapter 3.)

Assuming this returns the right figure, enter a similar formula into cells C3 and D3, with the column offset number suitably changed to return the right discount factor for the different manufacturing rates. Delete the entry in cell A3, ignore the error messages that suddenly appear, and create the data table exactly as before. For good measure, the labour costs can be added, as can the total cost which is the sum of parts and labour. The spreadsheet is complete.

What could have been a potentially error-prone and time consuming job if done by hand has just been completed quickly, easily, and without the risk of error.

In much the same way, any situation which calls for a variety of figures to be calculated in a variety of ways with a variety of formulas can best be done with a data table. It is even possible for those formulas to include references to other formulas, lookup tables or databases. Add to this the fact that those input values could also be the result of formulas or values from lookup tables and databases and it becomes apparent just how useful data tables can be.

In fact the only problem with data tables as they have been used so far is that they change only one value in the formula. No matter how many formulas there might be, the only value which is allowed to change is the input value. Everything else must remain the same. In many cases this is all that will be needed, but on other occasions there could be two values to be changed and for that you must use what is known as a two-way data table.

Before starting, a good tip is to enter a value into the input cell. It will have to be removed before the data table is calculated because the input cell must always be blank, but until then it gives any formulas something to work on when they reference that input cell. In this way the formula will return a value which can be confirmed as correct rather than an error message which could just as easily be a mistake with the formula and not the result of referring to an empty cell. In other words, prove the formula works, then delete the value in the input cell before creating the data table.

Two-way data tables

These are different to the one-way data table as described above in that where the one-way table has one input and many formulas, the two-way table has two input values but only one formula. Other than that, their creation and operation are virtually identical.

Take Figure 5.4. It shows a range of values in pounds sterling and then converts them into dollars and euros at various exchange rates. The only difference is that in this case just one formula is used, although it does call for two input cells.

	A	B	C	D	E	F	G
1							
2							
3			0	£5,000	£5,500	£6,000	
4			1.5	$7,500	$8,250	$9,000	
5		DOLLAR	1.6	$8,000	$8,800	$9,600	
6			1.7	$8,500	$9,350	$10,200	
7			0.5	€ 2,500	€ 2,750	€ 3,000	
8		EURO	0.6	€ 3,000	€ 3,300	€ 3,600	
9			0.7	€ 3,500	€ 3,850	€ 4,200	
10							

Figure 5.4 A conversion table using just one formula

While these input cells could be anywhere on the spreadsheet, here they have been designated as C2 for the column input and D2 for the row input. (Being blank there is nothing to signify this on the spreadsheet as shown.) That means the formula to be entered into cell C3 is:

```
=C2*D2
```

After that the data table can be created in the usual way except that in Excel both the column and row input cell references should be entered into the dialog box. In Lotus, when its dialog box appears first select Two-way data table and then enter both the input cell references.

Differences

In the previous example with the lookup table one single value was manipulated in various ways by the use of different formulas. Ignoring the fact that the input values were references to a lookup table, that is essentially what happened. However, in the last example, which used a two-way table, only one formula was entered, but that formula referred to two sets of values which were manipulated together according to that formula. An obvious example of how this could be used would be a row showing money to be borrowed and a column showing various interest rates. A two-way data table could then be used to calculate the repayments for every amount shown against every interest rate shown.

When it comes to the analysis of data, both types of data table have their uses. Which one to use will depend on how your data is to be analysed.

Scenario manager

Also known as version manager this is, as the name suggests, a way of presenting different versions or scenarios of the same set of figures so their effect on the data as a whole can be seen. What this means is when a spreadsheet is based on estimates, there has to be some mechanism which shows what happens when those estimates vary. For example, an estimate of sales could be something like 35,000–50,000 units, which is fine, except the income based on sales of 35,000 will be very different to that based on sales of 50,000. The question is, which of those sales figures should be shown on the spreadsheet?

The obvious answer is both and perhaps a few more besides, which is where scenario managers come in. They provide a mechanism for showing what effect the different estimates would have.

To explain this further, look at Table 5.1. This shows three estimates: best case, worst case and expected. Each one would have an impact on any spreadsheet that included them, but they could not all be shown at once; the spreadsheet would be too confusing. Instead a scenario or version manager should be used.

Table 5.1 Three different estimates

	Best Case	**Worst Case**	**Expected**
Income	£65,000	£35,000	£45,000
Expenditure	£35,000	£45,000	£40,000

A scenario manager allows more than one value to be stored in a single cell so these values can be swapped over almost literally at the touch of a button. One set of values could be best case, another worst case, and so on. As these values change, so too will the results of any other calculations based on those cells, which has the effect of changing all the results for that spreadsheet – and in the process shows the impact of different estimates so decisions can be taken accordingly.

This is also easy to do even if the process varies between the spreadsheets. To begin with, however, take any three cells on a blank spreadsheet, designate one as income, the second as expenditure and the third as profit. The cell for profit needs a formula to subtract expenditure from income, but, apart from that, everything is ready to create a few different versions of the same situation.

In Excel

From the menu select Tools, Scenario and then from the dialog box that appears select Add. Name this particular scenario 'Best', enter the references for the cells which are to be income and expenditure, then enter the best case values for those cells as shown in the table. Clicking on Show will enter those values into the spreadsheet. Now repeat the process and name the next scenario 'Worst'. Once the values are entered, clicking on Show will change the values in the relevant cells and will also change the calculated value in the profit cell. You can enter and then select as many scenarios as you need by clicking on Tool, Scenario, Show.

In Lotus

From the menu select Range, Version, New Version. In the dialog box that appears enter the name 'Best' and then enter the cell references for income and expenditure. Those cells will now have a box around them which includes a drop-down menu. Into the relevant cells enter the values for the best case version as shown in Table 5.1. Right-click on the drop-down menu, select New

If the box and its drop-down menu are too obtrusive, select Hide Version Name and Border from the menu and it will disappear.

Version and repeat the process, this time naming it 'Worst' and using the worst case figures. After that, clicking on this menu will show all the available versions which, when selected, will change the figures in the income and expenditure cells as well as changing the figure in the calculated profit cell. To add more versions simply repeat the process.

The different versions can be shown by selecting Display Version from the menu system at the top of the screen.

Whichever spreadsheet you are using, you can change as many cells as you need to provide a quick and easy way of changing figures to assess their impact.

Goal seeking

This is a useful facility built into all spreadsheets which in some ways reverses the normal procedure. Where under normal circumstances figures would be entered into a spreadsheet to give an answer depending on the formula being used, in goal seeking the answer is entered and the spreadsheet then works out what the figures must be to reach that answer, based on the same formula.

From this it can be seen that for a spreadsheet to do its job it requires three items of information:

■ a value which it must try to achieve;

■ a formula which it must follow when trying to achieve that value;

■ a cell whose value can be altered so that when used by the formula it will produce the desired result.

Excel goal seeking

Like databases, the goal seeking facilities in Excel can be described as either the simplest or the most primitive. It all depends on your point of view. Consider the spreadsheet in Figure 5.5. This shows a very simple example of goal seeking. The idea is that it shows the cost of a product and the foreign exchange rate so that the selling price (SP) in that country is calculated by the formula:

```
=C2*C4
```

	A	B	C	D
1				
2		Cost	26.50	
3				
4		Exchange	12.5	
5				
6		S.P.	331.25	
7				

Figure 5.5 A simple example of goal seeking in Excel

Now assume that the target selling price is actually 280.00 and not 331.25, which raises the question: What will the cost have to be to meet that target price at that exchange rate? Goal seeking can easily answer this question.

From the menu select Tools and then Goal Seek. A dialog box will appear which asks for three items of information:

- **Set Cell**. This cell must contain the formula which Excel will use in goal seeking. In this case that will be C6.
- **To Value**. This is the target value that Excel must try to achieve. In this case enter 280.0. For future reference the cell must contain a value only. It cannot contain a formula.
- **By changing cell**. This is the cell whose value will be changed. In this example it will be C2. For future reference, only one cell can be used. The spreadsheet cannot goal seek by changing more than one cell.

Once this information is entered, click on OK and Excel will automatically calculate the new cost to be 22.4 (assuming the cell has been formatted to one decimal places).

Lotus goal seeking

In Lotus, goal seeking is known as backsolving, although before any more is explained it would be best to consider the spreadsheet in Figure 5.6.

Although similar to the Excel spreadsheet this is slightly different to accommodate the extra facilities which Lotus offers. This shows the total cost of a product, a foreign exchange rate and the selling price (SP) of that product in foreign currency. The cost and admin values are as shown. The total is, obviously, the sum of those two which means the formula for the selling price is:

```
=C5*C8
```

A	A	B	C	D
1				
2		Cost	26.5	
3		Admin	12.6	
4				
5		Total	39.1	
6				
7				
8		Exchange	12.5	
9				
10		S.P.	488.75	
11				

Figure 5.6 Goal seeking in Lotus

Now suppose that the target selling price for that product is actually 380.0 and not the 488.75 it currently is, which raises the question: What must the costs actually be to meet the target price at that exchange rate? Goal seeking or backsolving can easily answer this question.

From the Range menu select Analyse, then Backsolver. A dialog box will appear which requires certain information to be entered into it. This will be:

- **Make formula in cell**. This calls for the reference of the cell holding the formula which Lotus 123 will use to do the backsolving. Here this will be cell C10.

- **Equal to**. This is the target value that Lotus must try to achieve. Enter the value 380.0.

- **By changing cell(s)**. This is the reference to the cell or cells which can be changed to meet the target value. Here enter the cells C2:C3.

The spreadsheet will now calculate the new values for cost and admin to be 20.6 and 9.8 respectively (at least, it will if the cells have been formatted to a single decimal place).

Although the formula in C10 actually referred to, among others, C5, it was this cell that referred to those cells that could be changed (C2:C3). In Lotus this is possible, but it must be done with care. While the formula that will be used in the backsolving process need not directly refer to the cell or cells that can be changed, the spreadsheet must still be told exactly what these cells are. In this case entering C5 as the cell to be changed would only confuse the spreadsheet. (It would change the value of cell C5 to meet the target value, but then the formula stored in C5 – the sum of C2 and C3 – would promptly return it to its original value. This explains why cells C2 and C3 had to be changed.)

If more than one cell, or set of values, is to be changed, Lotus works out what proportion of the total each value contributes and then changes each figure on a pro rata basis. Whatever the new total is, those figures will still be in the same proportion to it.

As we have seen, spreadsheets offer some powerful analysis tools, particularly as each one can be used in conjunction with the others or with any other function. Figures can be made more meaningful and more understandable by the application of the techniques described above.

Forecasting 6

Previous week actual

N week moving average

Exponential smoothing

Regression analysis

Forecasting is the methods used to decide the outcome of future events based on past results. Whether it is the number of passengers likely to buy a train ticket, the number of sales likely to be made in a given week or the number of cars on a road, they can all be forecast from previous records – and in a number of ways.

There are four main ways of providing forecasts. These are:

- previous week actual
- N week moving average
- exponential smoothing
- regression analysis.

Previous week actual

As the name implies, this uses the figures for the previous week as a forecast for the following week (or period). Although crude, this can be surprisingly accurate provided that conditions are not too volatile, but, as no spreadsheet work is required, this will not be discussed here.

N week moving average

This calculates a moving average over the previous N weeks (or periods). Exactly what value is taken for N can in some ways be a matter of trial and error to see what works best, but there are some general guidelines.

- The larger the value for N, the lower the change in the forecast figure from period to period.
- The smaller the value for N, the more sensitive the forecast is to changes and trends.

- Typical values are 52, 13 and 4, ie a year, a quarter and a month. If there are any seasonal variations in the data, the value of N must be large enough to cover at least one full set of figures where these variations occur. Covering several sets of such figures is also an option.

Once the figures are entered into a spreadsheet, the whole process is a simple as using the AVERAGE function.

N week forecasting is very easy to calculate, but even so it does have disadvantages. For instance, it is best applied to circumstances where the figures are truly random. If there is a trend in the figures, then taking an average of previous weeks means the forecast will always lag behind the trend; leading to an over- or under-capacity depending on which way the trend is running. Not only that but untypically large or small figures will affect the entire calculation, both when they are included within the average and when they first fall outside the selected range of the N value. When that happens there will be a sudden jump in the value of the average calculated which may or may not cause problems, but should at least be known about.

Exponential smoothing

This is a method by which such trends can be taken into account. It works by taking a weighted average where the previous actual figure is multiplied by an error factor known as the smoothing constant. In statistical terms this is described by the formula:

$$Fn = Fn\text{-}1 + A(Pn\text{-}1 - Fn\text{-}1)$$

where:

- Fn is the forecast for week n
- A is the smoothing constant
- P is the actual usage

In spreadsheet terms this can be implemented extremely easily, as Figure 6.1 shows.

	A	B	C	D	E	F
1			**Actual**		**Forecast**	
2		**Previous**	65		64	
3						
4			**Constant**			
5			**0.1**			
6						
7		**Current**			**64.1**	
8						

Figure 6.1 A basic spreadsheet for exponential smoothing

All it takes is the actual and forecast figures for the previous week, or period, and one simple formula to be entered into cell E7, namely:

    =E2+C5*(C2-E2)

The previous week's actual can be either entered manually or, as it will probably exist elsewhere, be entered by use of a database search in exactly the same way as the figures were obtained when calculating an N week moving average. Other than that the only point worth making concerns the value of the smoothing constant. While this can be any value, the recommended steps to follow are:

- use a value between 0.3 and 0.5 until a new pattern is established;
- then use a value of 0.1.

In general terms, the steeper the trend, the larger the value of the smoothing constant should be (ie closer to 0.5 than 0.3).

Regression analysis

This is by far the most scientific of all the forecasting methods. Not only can it produce an accurate assessment of future events, in as far as this is possible when basing the calculations on past results, it can also identify and compensate for any seasonal variations in whatever figures are being used. Of course, that also makes it more complex than any other forecasting method and so, for the sake of simplicity, the best idea is to take it in stages, starting with seasonal variations.

Seasonal variations

Although variations due to the seasons are by far the most common there could equally be times when the figures are affected by some other cyclical activity. There will always be events – sunspots, stock market crashes or flu epidemics – which do not easily fit into an annual, or seasonal, time scale, yet which still need to be calculated. To make matters even more complicated, it might well be that another trend is hidden among the seasonal or cyclical variations which also has to be both detected and calculated. Fortunately this can be done, although it does involve slightly more than a simple menu command or function. Instead an entirely different spreadsheet needs to be created and a new method has to be learned.

This process is known as decomposition because it breaks down, or decomposes, the figures into their constituent parts: the base figure, a trend value and a seasonal component. Each of these is then calculated separately before being recombined to produce the forecast, although how they are combined depends on the results of the decomposition process. If the figures are fairly stable, the trend and seasonal values are simply added to the base value which is known as the additive model. On the other hand, if there is a distinct trend apparent within the figures, then the seasonal component is multiplied by the trend value as it is assumed that the seasonal variation will also increase by the same rate as the trend. This figure will then be added to the base value and is known as a multiplicative model.

Let's start by considering the spreadsheet in Figure 6.2. This shows a forecast made by a railway company to predict the number of tickets likely to be sold and is begun by entering the year and quarter number followed by the actual tickets sold in previous years. All the rest will be calculated.

The first step with any such forecast is to remove the seasonal variations by taking the moving average of four complete quarters or seasons. The fact that these four quarters are not all from the same year is irrelevant; what counts is that together they make up a complete annual cycle and collectively cancel out any variations due to seasonal or other factors. That being the case, the formula to be entered into cell D8 is:

If some other cyclical event was being measured that had a different number of periods, the range over which the average was taken would obviously have to accommodate this.

```
=AVERAGE(C5:C11)
```

This formula must then be entered into all the relevant cells in the spreadsheet, which can best be done by copying it to the clipboard and then pasting it back to the various cells. The cell references will be changed accordingly and the correct moving average will be taken in every case.

	A	B	C	D	E	F
1		**A Railway Co Ltd**				
2		Passenger Forecast				
3						
4	Year	Quarter	Tickets sold	Moving Avg	Seasonally adjusted value	Seasonal Index
5	1995	3	2268			
6						
7	1995	4	1963			
8				2159		
9	1996	1	2019		2173	0.929077
10				2188		
11	1996	2	2385		2216	1.076385
12				2244		
13	1996	3	2383		2259	1.055125
14				2273		
15	1996	4	2189		2287	0.957149
16				2301		
17	1997	1	2135		2374	0.899515
18				2446		
19	1997	2	2497		2480	1.007007
20				2513		
21	1997	3	2963		2548	1.162816
22				2583		
23	1997	4	2458		2591	0.94876
24				2599		
25	1998	1	2414		2602	0.927837
26				2605		
27	1998	2	2559		2610	0.98046
28				2615		
29	1998	3	2989		2621	1.140622
30				2626		
31	1998	4	2498		2636	0.947783
32				2645		
33	1999	1	2458			
34						
35	1999	2	2636			
36						
37	1999	3				
38						
39	1999	4				

Figure 6.2 A forecast of the number of rail tickets likely to be sold

To bring the figures in line with the quarter is known in the jargon as centring them on the quarter.

The whole point of the exercise is to remove any seasonal variations from the figures by taking a moving average over four quarters.

The only problem with this is that a moving average will always lag behind any trends which might be present in the figures and is, anyway, not representative of any particular quarter. Being what is known as a four-point moving average there will always be two data points behind the quarter in question. Therefore, to bring the figures in line with the quarter, the trick is to take a moving average of the moving average. This means that the formula for cell E9 is:

    =AVERAGE(D8:D10)

This averages the figures on either side of a quarter, which are themselves averages, to produce a figure which as far as possible equates to an actual value for that quarter once any quarterly – or seasonal – variations have been removed.

Unfortunately, if these moving averages are to be used for detecting and calculating trends, which they are, then the fact that two of the four figures used to produce that average are behind each particular quarter means the trend will be that much harder to spot. Two quarters ago the trend might not have appeared. To counter this, take the average of the figures on either side of the quarter in question and use this to calculate any trends.

If something other than quarterly results is being measured, what happens depends entirely on how many periods make up one complete cycle. For example, if the year has been split into three, just take the simple moving average. Similarly, a five-period cycle can be treated in the same way and for the same reason. In both cases one of the figures being used to calculate that average is centred exactly on the period. That may sound confusing, but look at the spreadsheet. To show the moving average correctly positioned between the four quarters it is averaging it must be placed on a row between two of those quarterly figures. If the average was for only three or five figures, it would be placed on the same row.

From this a crude, but workable rule of thumb can be followed. If the average can be shown on the same line as one of the figures it is averaging, then no more need be done. Alternatively, if it has to be shown on a line between two of the figures, take the average of the average. As the spreadsheet shows, every figure on the seasonally adjusted column is on exactly the same row as the quarter numbers. This can then be used in future calculations.

Exactly what those calculations will be depends entirely on whether or not there is a trend hidden within those figures. If the differences between each quarter's, or each period's, figures are due entirely to seasonal variation, one set of calculations must be performed. Alternatively, if there is a rising or falling demand hidden within those variations, another set of calculations are needed. This makes the next step obvious: find out if a trend exists.

The easiest way is to produce an XY or scatter graph based on the results of the seasonally adjusted values (column E in Figure 6.2). To do this, copy the results to some other part of the spreadsheet where they can be shown without the blank rows in between. This will be the Y, or dependent, axis. The X axis is created by numbering the cells in the next column, starting at 1 and ending at whatever number corresponds to the last entry for the Y axis. In the example this would be as shown in Figure 6.3.

Despite appearances these are the same seasonally adjusted figures as appear in column E. The difference is caused entirely by the fact that one group of cells has been formatted to zero decimal places which, as we have seen already, makes no difference to the result of any calculations.

	I	J
6		
7	1	2173.125
8	2	2215.75
9	3	2258.5
10	4	2287
11	5	2373.5
12	6	2479.625
13	7	2548.125
14	8	2590.75
15	9	2601.75
16	10	2610
17	11	2620.5
18	12	2635.625

Figure 6.3 Creating an XY graph

Once the values have been copied, and once every value has a number associated with it as per the example, create the graph. Then add a trend line and see what happens.

If there is no trend, the additive model applies. This, paradoxically, is calculated by first subtracting the seasonally adjusted value from the actual ticket sales per quarter which, if no trend were apparent, would make the formula in F9:

```
=C9-E9
```

However, as there is a trend in these figures, the multiplicative model applies and as this involves first dividing the actual figures by the adjusted value, the formula should actually be:

```
=C9/E9
```

Once again this should be copied, or pasted, into all the relevant cells as shown on the spreadsheet.

What happens after that is the same no matter what model is used. While the figures in column F show a trend value which varies over time, what is needed is just one single index value for each of the four quarters which will form the basis for all future calculations. What those calculations are, and why only one figure is needed, will be made clear later, but for the time being concentrate on producing those quarterly index figures. This is done by taking the average of each quarterly seasonal index so that all the averages for quarter 1 are averaged, as are those for quarter 2, and so on. In terms of Figure 6.2 this means taking a blank cell, say B43, and into it entering the formula:

```
=AVERAGE(F9+F17+F25)
```

You can see that the cell references all correspond to the first quarter. From this it should be apparent that similar formulas need to be entered to calculate the index value for the other three quarters to produce a result like that shown in Figure 6.4.

To recap. Quarterly sales of railway tickets were entered into a spreadsheet. The seasonal element within those quarterly sales was removed and the base figures left were tested to see if a trend was apparent. The multiplicative model was used to, eventually, produce an index figure for each of the four quarters.

The information is now available to start forecasting ticket sales for the remainder of 1999.

	A	B
42		
43	Q1	0.91881
44	Q2	1.021284
45	Q3	1.119521
46	Q4	0.951231
47		

Figure 6.4 Calculating the index value

Just to show how useful spreadsheets can be there is a function called FORE-CAST which does exactly what its name suggests. All you need to do is enter the right information into its arguments. Before then, so the process can make more sense, take another look at the cells which were used to create the XY graph. Down one column are the numbers 1 to 12 with the seasonally adjusted values beside them. Now imagine that the figure 13 was entered and the spreadsheet magically calculated the appropriate value beside it. That is what the FORECAST function does. In effect this is the same as the trend line that is produced with the XY graph. The spreadsheet projects the trend line forward and then, in the case of this function, shows what the figure would be to create it. (Exactly how it does this will be explained at the end of the chapter.)

To show that in action enter the figure 13 into cell I19 (see Figure 6.3), assuming this is the column that was used to produce the graph. Then, in cell J19, the function can be entered. In both Lotus and Excel this has three arguments:

- **X.** In effect the next number in the sequence – 13, or cell reference I19, in this case.

- **Known Y's.** The numbers which had previously been used to show the trend line; in this case J7:J18.
- **Known X's.** The previous numbers in the sequence; in this case cells I7:I18.

It therefore follows that the formula to be entered into cell J19 is:

```
=FORECAST(I19,J7:J18,I7:I18)
```

Assuming everything has gone smoothly, this should show the figure 2755.992 as the next seasonally adjusted figure. All you then need to do is to enter the figures 14, 15 and 16 into the correct cells and the entire process can be repeated to show the figure for each of the four quarters. Once again assuming everything has gone according to plan, these figures should be 2803.142, 2850.291 and 2897.441.

Since these figures represent the forecasted seasonally adjusted figures for the four quarters of 1999, they can then be transferred into the relevant section of the spreadsheet. In other words, the formula for cell E33 is simply:

```
=J19
```

Similarly, the values in cells J20, J21 and J22 can be transferred to cells E35, E37 and E39 respectively.

Once those figures are in place they can be used together with the seasonal index to calculate future ticket sales.

This is where additive or multiplicative models finally start living up to their names. If there is no trend, the additive model is used, which means that the number of ticket sales is the seasonally adjusted value, as has just been calcu-

For those who tried copying the formula down into cells J20 to J22 and now have different answers, the cell references for the Known Y's and Known X's should have been made absolute first. Doing this should produce the right figures.

In fact the FORECAST function could have been entered directly into these cells; it was just done this way to make the process more understandable.

lated, plus the relevant quarterly index. If a trend has been shown, the formula is the seasonally adjusted value multiplied by the quarterly index. This means that the formula for cell C37 is:

```
=E37*B45
```

This should also make the formula in C39 obvious so, once that is entered, it can be seen that the forecasted ticket sales for the third and fourth quarters of 1999 are 3191 and 2756 respectively (when formatted to zero decimal places, naturally).

The reason for having two different models – additive and multiplicative – is relatively simple. If there is no trend, the differences between the quarters are due entirely to cyclical factors such as the main holiday period or the Christmas rush – the normal reasons why sales of any product might vary. Under these circumstances once the new values are calculated it simply becomes a matter of adding the seasonal factors to these values to complete the forecast.

Keep in mind that the quarterly index is no more than a measure of how sales within a quarter are affected by any seasonal factors and it should make sense. For any product affected by seasonal variations there will always be a base line sales figure plus an additional amount which represents those seasonal variations. The seasonally adjusted figure represents the base line, with the quarterly index being the amount that has to be added due to seasonal factors.

On the other hand, when there is a trend in the figures, either upwards or downwards, something different has to be done for that very reason. The results for one quarter will no longer be roughly similar to the same quarter in the previous year. They will be greater or smaller depending on which way the trend is running and it is this that the multiplicative model calculates.

In broad terms, forecasting a trend calls for the base line figures plus any seasonal variations plus an amount equal to that trend. If the trend is rising at 10%, then the final figure, base line plus seasonal variation, must be increased by the same 10%. This is handled by the multiplicative model. The quarterly, or period, index and the trend factor are incorporated into one figure which, when multiplied by the base line, or seasonally adjusted, value gives the forecast for the period in question.

But what happens if the figures are influenced by more than one factor? This is known as multiple regression.

Multiple regression
Again this seems difficult only because of the terminology used. Consider Table 6.1. This shows the growth rate of a plant which is influenced both by the amount of rain that fell on it and the amount of sunlight it received. In other words it is affected by two factors which together determine its growth. The

Table 6.1 Factors influencing a plant's growth

Growth (cms)	Rain (cms)	Sun (hrs)
2.1	1.3	4.2
1.9	1.1	3.9
2.3	1.4	4.4
2.2	1.2	4.1
?	0.9	3.7

question is, if these two factors are known, can its growth be predicted? The answer is, yes, easily, even if the regression analysis must now be performed on multiple coefficients.

To start making sense of all this look at the spreadsheet in Figure 6.5. This is the same as Table 6.1 with the exception of cell A6 which is the result of the forecast. Again, the method varies slightly between the spreadsheets:

- In **Lotus**, select Range, Analyse, Regression.
- In **Excel**, start with the Tools menu. If the Data Analysis option is there use that, if not it must be loaded from the CD-ROM. To do that select Add-Ins and then click on Data Analysis. After that Microsoft provides enough built-in help to make the process quick and relatively painless. Once that is done, the Data Analysis option will appear on the menu and from there the Regression option can be chosen.

One of the other options will be Histogram, but this is best ignored. Despite its name, all it does is to sort a list of figures into frequency ranges in exactly the same way as the FREQUENCY function.

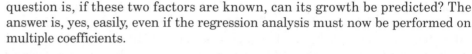

	A	B	C
1	Growth (cms)	Rain (cms)	Sun (Hrs)
2	2.1	1.3	4.2
3	1.9	1.1	3.9
4	2.3	1.4	4.4
5	2.2	1.2	4.1
6	2.1	0.9	3.7
7			

Figure 6.5 Information from Table 6.1 with the result of the forecast

No matter what the spreadsheet, the next step is to enter the X and Y ranges into the dialog box that appears. In this example, of course, the X range is B2:C5 as these are the independent variables. (The sun will still shine and the rain will still fall no matter how fast the plants grow.) Equally, the Y range is A2:A5 as this is the dependent variable. (Plant growth depends entirely on sun and rain.) Once that is done an output area needs to be defined which should be at least seven columns wide and seven rows deep. Why this is necessary becomes obvious as soon as the OK button is clicked because one of the following will appear (Figure 6.6).

LOTUS

C	F	G	H	I
9				
10		Regression Output:		
11	Constant			-6.775
12	Std Err of Y Est			0.05
13	R Squared			0.971429
14	No. of Observations			4
15	Degrees of Freedom			1
16				
17	X Coefficient(s)		-4.5	3.5
18	Std Err of Coef.		1.802776	1.118034
19				

EXCEL

	F	G
30	SUMMARY OUTPUT	
31		
32	Regression Statistics	
33	Multiple R	0.985610761
34	R Square	0.971428571
35	Adjusted R Square	0.914285714
36	Standard Error	0.05
37	Observations	4
38		
39	ANOVA	
40		df
41	Regression	2
42	Residual	1
43	Total	3
44		
45		Coefficients
46	Intercept	-6.775
47	X Variable 1	-4.5
48	X Variable 2	3.5
49		

Figure 6.6 The output areas in Lotus and Excel

A lot more will appear in Excel, but this is the part that concerns forecasting so the rest has been ignored.

To carry out this forecasting the calculations are:

First X value multiplied by the first X coefficient

Plus

Second X value multiplied by the second X coefficient

Plus

The Constant or Intercept value

Without using cell references which might be different depending on where the output table appears on a spreadsheet, the first X value is 0.9 (B6 on that part of the spreadsheet where the cell references should be the same) which is to be multiplied by –4.5. Similarly, the second X value is 4.1 which is multiplied by 3.5 and the constant or intercept is –6.775. The sum of all these calculations will then return the value as shown in cell A6 which is, of course, the forecast for plant growth.

Applied regression analysis

All the techniques covered so far have calculated like for like. Previous sales of rail tickets have been used to forecast future ticket sales. While this may form the basis for most forecasting, there will be times when something more is needed. An example here would be the sale of accessories or supplementary products. If the sale of, say, cameras can be predicted, can the same figures be used to predict the sale of camera accessories or insurance policies for that camera, or anything else that may be bought alongside that main item?

To put that into a statistical context, can a relationship be found between two figures so that the value of one can be used to predict the value of the other and if so, how much can that forecast be relied on?

Perhaps unsurprisingly the answer lies in applied regression analysis. Consider the spreadsheet in Figure 6.7. This shows the sales of a piece of industrial equipment which can be supplied with any one of three different sets of tooling depending on the application it will be used for. The question here is not only can the machine sales for the following month be predicted, but also can the same be done for the different sets of tooling?

	A	B	C	D	E
13					
14	Month	Machine sales	Tooling A	Tooling B	Tooling C
15	1	124	74	31	19
16	2	131	79	33	19
17	3	127	76	32	19
18	4	119	71	30	18
19	5	128	77	32	19
20	6	132	79	33	20
21					

Figure 6.7 Sales of a piece of industrial equipment

This may seem like the opposite of the previous example where two known figures were used to produce an estimate for a third, but in fact there is very little difference. They both use the same methods, although in this case regression analysis is taken a little bit further to demonstrate how valuable it can be as a forecasting tool.

To start with, consider the spreadsheet in Figure 6.8. This shows the forecast only for Tooling A on the grounds that as the process is exactly the same for Tooling B and Tooling C they can be omitted for the sake of simplicity. First the machine sales have to be calculated which, again for the sake of simplicity, was done by taking the average of the previous six months (ie a six-period moving average) to make the formula in cell B5:

=AVERAGE(B15:B20)

	A	B	C	D	E
1			Forecast		
2					
3				Tooling A	
4		Machine Sales	Highest	Mid	Lowest
5		127	79	76	73
6					

Figure 6.8 The forecast for Tooling A

After that the tooling sales can be calculated, which is done not by using the FORECAST function but by choosing the Regression option wherever it might be found on a particular spreadsheet. Use cells B15:B20 as the X variable and cells C15:C20 as the Y, then produce the output summary as before. Unfortunately, because different spreadsheets arrange the summary in different ways, it is difficult to describe the next part of the process in terms of cell references. For that reason a description is all that can be used, but it still should be relatively easy to convert those into cell references. As such the formula for D5 is:

=B5 * X Variable [X Coefficient] + Intercept [Constant]

The first description is for Excel; the descriptions in brackets are for Lotus users.

This is exactly as we have done before and should return the value shown. Then it is time to consider the next likely question: If this is the mid value, how are the highest and lowest values calculated?

This goes back to what we said earlier about the accuracy of these forecasts. As any forecast, or any estimate, can never be totally accurate, there has to be a margin of error built into any forecast. In regression analysis that margin of error is referred to as the standard error of coefficient, which is a technical-sounding name for something that can be used easily. All it really involves is including this standard error in the formula; adding it to the X coefficient to produce the highest possible figure and subtracting it to produce the lowest. To show it in action the formula for cell C5 is:

```
=B5*(X Variable [X Coefficient] + Standard Error) + Intercept [Constant]
```

Once again the descriptions for Lotus users are in the square brackets. The round brackets are needed in either spreadsheet because of the order of precedence. The standard error must be added to the X value before the total is multiplied by B5. That apart, there should be no problem in finding the right cell in the output summary, although if it helps the value is 0.026125.

After that the results practically speak for themselves. The true forecast for sales of Tooling A is actually somewhere between 73 and 79, with the mid point being 76.

Regression analysis can be that versatile. Instead of just returning one value of an estimate, the highest, lowest and mid points can all be returned for use in such things as the version or scenario managers mentioned previously.

It should also be fairly obvious that the formula for cell E5 is exactly the same, apart from the fact that here the standard error should be subtracted from the X variable/coefficient.

Alternatively, the range over which the values could vary can be used in what if data table calculations. Once you have mastered the technique the only surprise will be how often you can use it.

Of course, one final question must also be answered: How strong is the relationship between the two sets of figures which make up the X and Y coefficients?

Strength of relationship
In non-technical terms this simply means how reliable will the forecast be; how strong is the link between the two sets of figures? This is shown by the R squared value which is also returned as part of the output summary and can be defined as follows:

0.0 **To** 0.2   Negligible

0.2 **To** 0.4   Weak

0.4 **To** 0.7   Moderate

0.7 **To** 0.9   Strong

0.9 **To** 1.0   Very Strong

In the example the relationship between machine sales and Tooling A has an R squared value of 0.993469, so the strength of the relationship can easily be seen. In this or in any other set of figures a strong or very strong relationship means there is a direct link between the values in question – changes in one figure are **directly and exclusively** caused by changes in the other. A lower value means that other factors are involved. Exactly what this other factor, or factors, might be obviously depends on the situation, but the point is once they are known to exist they can be searched for. Until regression analysis was performed they could well have been overlooked.

Regression analysis

7

A brief overview

A brief overview

Regression analysis is a mathematical technique for determining whether a relationship exists between two sets of figures, known as the dependent and independent variable and, if so, whether that relationship can be used to calculate future values of that dependent variable. To demonstrate how it works, suppose that the two sets of figures are as shown below:

Dependent Variable	Independent Variable
4	2
4	3
5	6
6	8
7	10

Any future values of the dependent variable can then be calculated by the formula:

Y = A + B*X

Of course, before this formula can be used values must be found for A and B which involves two, much bigger, formulas:

$$A = \bar{Y} \, \frac{\sum(X - \bar{X})(Y - \bar{Y})\bar{X}}{\sum(X - \bar{X})^2}$$

$$B = \frac{\sum(X - \bar{X})(Y - \bar{Y})}{\sum(X - \bar{X})^2}$$

where $\sum$ means the sum of, and $\bar{X}$ and $\bar{Y}$ mean the average value of X and Y, which in the case of the above figures is 5.8 and 5.4 respectively. This would, therefore, give the results shown in Table 7.1.

Table 7.1 Regression analysis

X	Y	$X-\bar{X}$	$Y-\bar{Y}$	$(X-\bar{X})(Y-\bar{Y})$	$(X-\bar{X})^2$
4	2	−3.8	−1.4	5.3	14.4
4	3	−2.8	−1.4	3.9	7.8
6	6	0.2	0.6	0.1	0.1
7	8	2.2	1.6	3.5	4.8
6	10	4.2	0.6	2.5	17.6
Total 27	**29**	**0**	**0**	**15.3**	**44.7**

The fact that $X-\bar{X}$ and $Y-\bar{Y}$ both total zero can be explained easily. Were all of the figures in Table 7.1 plotted on a graph, it would be impossible to draw a straight line that connects, or even comes close to, them all. The best that could be done would be to draw a line that comes as close as possible to as many of them as possible. Assuming that was done and the difference between the line and each point calculated, the sum of those calculations would be zero. It would have to be. Where the line was below a certain point the difference between them would calculate to a negative figure (the value as represented by the line would be less than the value of that particular point). Similarly where the line was above a point the figure would be positive so that when all the differences were calculated the sum would be zero. If not, the line would not be equally distant from all the points.

Returning to the example, if these figures are applied to the formulas that would give:

$$A = 5.4 - \frac{15.3 * 5.8}{44.7} = 3.4$$

$$B = \frac{15.3}{44.7} = 0.3$$

This means that the formula for calculating a new value for Y is:

$$Y = 3.4 + 0.3 * X$$

Nevertheless, while regression analysis is not difficult to understand or to calculate, it is still a lot quicker to use the built-in spreadsheet functions.

Simulation 8

State the requirements

Analyse the system

Formulate the mathematical model

Create the simulation

Verify the simulation

Carry out the simulation

There is a wide variety of specialist software packages for simulation, yet a great deal of useful work can still be done with a spreadsheet. There may not be a menu option available, but it can still be done.

All you need to do is accept that there will be figures on a screen which represent the different elements of whatever system is being simulated in exactly the same way that the figures in a budget forecast represent cash in the bank.

In the minds of most people computer simulation, sometimes known as computer modelling, means scientists in white coats staring at animated displays of sub-atomic particles or something equally incomprehensible. Certainly few people would believe it could have any application in the real world, or that it could be done using nothing more than a spreadsheet.

The first thing to realise is that almost anything could be considered a simulation. For example, a budget forecast or a cash flow analysis could be described as a simulation of events yet to happen. They both take a combination of expected circumstances and project forward to show a future result. In essence, all simulation does this. The only difference is that such things as cash flow calculations are based on known events and are, therefore, described as being deterministic: the same starting conditions will always produce the same results. True simulation, on the other hand, involves a random element and is known as stochastic.

Simulation is nothing more than working out the mathematical relationship between a variety of elements and then creating a formula so that entering one figure (representing one element) produces another (representing a different element). In practical terms, it could mean deciding that the selling price of a product is cost plus 15%. Therefore, a mathematical relationship has been defined and a formula can be created so that entering the cost figure means the profit will be automatically calculated. And that is so similar to every other spreadsheet that everything else can be taken for granted.

So, why create a simulation?

- **To make assumptions explicit**. As a simulation requires precise mathematical formulas, vague assumptions and gut feelings are replaced with explicit figures which can then be tested.

- **To define the problem**. As there must be a logical relationship between everything being considered in the simulation this can, by itself, not only clarify the situation but also define the problem precisely.

- **To provide a frame of reference**. If a simulation is created at the beginning of a project, all future work can then be related back to that, both to help control the project and so that all those involved can see how one activity fits into the picture as a whole.

- **To provide answers to what if types of questions**. Once the simulation has been created, basic what if calculations can be performed to help predict the result of future actions.

- **To clearly express the results**. With simulation, everything can be expressed in financial terms, which is often the only kind of information that interests senior management.

- **To obtain an objective evaluation**. Since simulation is based on fact, not opinion, the personal bias or prejudice of others can be excluded. It can also be used to explain, or defend, the reasons behind a particular decision.

- **To resolve conflicts of interest**. Once the problem has been defined, areas of conflict can become apparent which can then be dealt with.

- **To minimise risk**. If the effects of different actions can be predicted in advance, the risks associated with those actions can be kept to a minimum.

With a list like that, just about anyone can find a use for simulation, no matter what their department, discipline or profession.

This brings us to how it can be done. There is an argument that deciding when to do it should be the first question, but without knowing the how, the when will make no sense. Only by understanding what has to be done is it possible to know when it is likely to be useful, as that way the possibilities and limitations of using a spreadsheet as a simulation tool can be properly appreciated. After that the question will practically answer itself, at least to the extent that those times when simulation is the appropriate technique will very likely be obvious.

So how is it done? In fact, no differently from any other spreadsheet, once a few conditions are met. Before you even need a computer you must first put in a great deal of work.

State the requirements

Simulation, like any other spreadsheet technique, is a means of answering questions, so first of all someone has to decide what those questions are. Usually this will involve trying to learn something about the system being simulated. For example, a simulation of traffic flow along a particular stretch of road might be done to discover the effects of different traffic management systems in which case that would be the question. Alternatively, given the flexibility of spreadsheet models, several different but related questions could be asked. Anything is possible, providing the questions are known before the simulation is designed.

Analyse the system

Find out how one part of the system works with, or against, another. Understand how each individual element fits into the system as a whole.

Talk to the people concerned and build a consensus about what the system can and cannot do, or should be doing.

This is not quite as difficult as it might sound because what it means is simply find out what is happening, or is likely to happen, before trying to simulate it inside a computer.

The next part is to establish the boundaries of the simulation. In other words, decide what is to be included and what can be safely left out. To take the traffic management example above, it could be argued that how traffic flows through one part of town depends on other traffic flows in other areas and yet, since simulating traffic patterns for the entire country is unfeasible, someone has to decide what is relevant and what can be ignored.

The best way of doing this is to keep in mind why the system is being simulated in the first place; what questions it is supposed to answer. If this is done the simulation will be neither so simplistic that important elements are overlooked, nor so complex that the whole project becomes bogged down in unnecessary details. Even so this can still be something of an art form as anyone creating a simulation should not only consider what questions it will be designed to answer but also what other questions might be asked of it at some later date.

For example, it is highly likely that a simulation set up to show the effects of interest rates on inflation would at some time also be expected to show the effects of those same interest rates on unemployment. So likely in fact that the simulation should be created to include unemployment from the beginning. Alternatively, of course, if the spreadsheet was created to predict the effects of increased advertising on sales of a particular product, then including the consequences of interest rates on high street spending would be to create something far more complex than was necessary.

Just remember, if a system cannot be understood, it cannot be simulated. So, strip the system to its barest essentials and start from there. Should other elements be needed they can always be added later. Even if it means completely rebuilding the spreadsheet, again and again, at least the finished result will resemble the system.

These might sound like obvious, if not extreme, examples, but they do give an indication of what to be aware of when systems are being analysed for later simulation.

Formulate the mathematical model

This means to create the formulas that will be entered into the spreadsheet later.

Jargon such as mathematical models might make the whole exercise seem highly technical, but in effect it is no more than would be done for any spreadsheet. It is only the jargon that is difficult; doing it is easy.

Define the relationships between the various items of data being entered, express that in the numerical or logical terms necessary for it to be accepted by a spreadsheet, then decide how the result should be displayed (ie will it be the total, the average, the maximum, the minimum, something else or a combination of them all?).

This is easy as long as the basic design rules are followed. In Chapter 1 we showed that any formula should be checked to see that it produces the right results even under extreme circumstances. This goes double for simulation. Since the whole point of simulation is to see how systems behave, very often at the extremes, if the formulas break down at this point the entire spreadsheet becomes useless. Checking for this at the design stage will save a lot of work later on – not to mention preventing faulty results leading to faulty decisions.

Create the simulation

Unsurprisingly this means to build the spreadsheet.

Verify the simulation

This is a double check of everything that has been done so far. First of all check that the formulas are producing the expected results, if necessary by using a calculator. Then confirm that the simulation itself is working correctly.

If the system being simulated is already in operation, historical data should be used in comparison with the results produced by the spreadsheet. That way, if the two are, broadly speaking, in line with each other, the accuracy of the simulation is confirmed.

Should this be a new system, or project, being simulated with no historical data to rely on, the only check available is to ask whether the results seem credible. This does not mean dismissing any strange results out of hand as very often simulation will produce surprises. Systems can work differently than expected when certain conditions are met and it is the function of simulation to highlight this. You should make sure that the simulation works as expected under normal conditions and that any anomalies can be explained. In other words, follow the logic through and confirm that everything works as it should.

Carry out the simulation

Once the spreadsheet (simulation) has been confirmed as accurate, it can be used to predict future results. Better yet, as the spreadsheet has been proven to be accurate, the results produced can be used with confidence. Even so, where the system itself is operating under conditions of uncertainty, it is best not to rely on the results gained by running the simulation only once. As no one can accurately predict the number of sales that will be made in a given day or the number of cars using a road in a given hour, there will always be uncertainty in any system, and this should be taken into account.

The recommended practice is to run the simulation several times and then to take an average of the results gained. In this way all conditions are likely to be tested and the simulation can be used with that much more confidence.

Let's take an example (Figure 8.1)

	A	B	C	D	E	F	G	H
1								
2	**Sales**			**Admin**			**Assembly**	
3	Process rate	80		Process Rate	60		Process rate	40
4	Employees F/T	8		Employees F/T	9		Employees F/T	12
5	Employees P/T	0		Employees P/T	3		Employees P/T	6
6	Capacity	640		Capacity	630		Capacity	600
7								
8								
9				**TELEPHONE SALES OPERATION**				
10				SYSTEM SIMULATION				
11								
12	Staff costs	£38.00					Estimated orders:	
13	Overhead	£2,750.00					Min	500
14	Total costs	£4,023.00					Max	750
15							Profit on order	£7.50
16								
17				Cost of lost sales	£3,352.50			
18				Admin backlog	20			
19				Assembly backlog	99			
20								
21				Profit	£17,325.00			
22								

Figure 8.1 A simulation of a proposed telephone sales operation

This shows what might be described as the control panel for a simulation of a proposed telephone sales operation. Under this system orders are received by the sales department which passes the details through to admin where credit checks are carried out and paperwork is raised. This then goes through to assembly where the orders are physically assembled and despatched. The process rate is the number of orders each person can process per day, with the part-time (P/T) workers achieving only half that rate.

The expected number of orders per day, and the expected profit per order, are as shown. Similarly, the staff costs are per full-time (F/T) employee per day. Part-time employees earn half that amount.

This, then, is the system which is to be simulated to find out not only the optimum staffing levels but also how those staffing levels could create what might be unacceptably high backlogs of orders in the admin or assembly departments. Not only that, as it is assumed that an order not taken is an order lost (if the phones are constantly engaged customers will go elsewhere), the simulation will also show the cost of those lost orders. Finally, it will show the profit that can be expected assuming these figures hold true.

How the simulation will do all of this will be explained later, but first consider the control panel or display. All the figures for sales, admin and assembly can be entered as shown, with the obvious exception of the capacity calculation which requires a formula. In this case the formula, for cell B6, is:

```
=INT(B3*B4+(B3/2)*B5)
```

Ignoring the INT function for a moment, this is simply the process rate multiplied by the number of full-time employees plus half the process rate multiplied by the number of part-time employees. The brackets are there simply to make the calculation work in the right way according to the rules of precedence.

If ever an application calls for only the numbers to the right of a decimal point to be returned the INT function can also be used. As an example 7.9-INT(7.9) would return the answer of 0.9.

The INT function takes any number or formula and returns only the integer part, the number to the left of the decimal point. It was used here because changes to the process rate and/or the number of employees could result in a capacity figure that ended with a decimal fraction, which would not reflect reality. No one accepts half or two-thirds of an order. The cell could have been formatted not to show any of these decimal fractions, but that affects the display only. They would still exist within the spreadsheet and would still be used in any future calculations, which could cause errors and even stranger looking figures. In much the same way the ROUND function was not used because that could round up to the next highest figure, which would mean something like 0.7 or 0.8 of an order being counted as complete when this would never be the case in real life.

The overhead figure represents all the other costs associated with running the operation. This is an example of defining the boundaries of a simulation. Only the day-to-day activities are to be considered, which puts everything else outside the boundary, but as these costs are needed before a final profit can be calculated, everything was lumped together into that one figure. In this way everything from equipment and building costs to supervisory salaries can be included in the final calculations without being considered as part of the simulation.

The total costs as shown in cell B14 is the number of full-time employees multiplied by the cost per day (in cell B12) plus the number of part-time employees multiplied by half the cost per day. The overhead costs are added to this, which means the formula for B14 is:

```
=B12*(B4+E4+H4)+B12/2*(B5+E5+H5)+B13
```

As the other figures will be added later once the simulation is run, the only other point to be mentioned is the display itself. This simply took all the information and separated it into logical groups to make the spreadsheet easier to understand. Although this should be done with any spreadsheet, it is even more important when simulations are involved because they are likely to be used by more people. Assuming a simulation is created as part of some project monitoring and control process, it is likely that all the project team members will have access to it, both to change the figures and to see the results of those changes. Therefore the easier it is to understand, the more likely it is that it will be used and the better it will repay the time spent on creating it.

The working part of the simulation

So let's create the working part of this simulation. First consider the spreadsheet in Figure 8.2 (see page 156).

After the explanation given so far the data labels should be self-explanatory, leaving just the formulas themselves to be considered.

First, the day numbers in column L are just that, numbers. Start at 1, fill the series down as far as 50 and the job is done. Then the sales figures can be calculated.

At the heart of this formula is a function known as RAND (or RND in some spreadsheets) which returns a random number somewhere between 0 and 1. How that becomes useful obviously depends on the rest of the formula, but before that let us look at RAND, which is not altogether straightforward.

This is not the complete spreadsheet, but as the mid section is just more of the same it was left out for the sake of convenience.

The first point to be aware of is that while a number between 0 and 1 will be returned at random, the number will never be exactly 1. In practice this means that multiplying the randomly generated number by 100, for example, will only

	L	M	N	O	P	Q
			Admin	**Assembly**	**No. of**	**Cost of**
2	**Day**	**Sales**	**Backlog**	**Backlog**	**lost sales**	**lost sales**
3	1	551	0	0	0	£0.00
4	2	604	0	4	0	£0.00
5	3	548	0	0	0	£0.00
6	4	543	0	0	0	£0.00
7	5	616	0	16	0	£0.00
8	6	531	0	0	0	£0.00
9	7	637	7	30	0	£0.00
10	8	586	0	16	0	£0.00
11	9	663	10	46	23	£172.50
12	10	710	20	76	70	£525.00

47	45	584	0	27	0	£0.00
48	46	743	10	57	103	£772.50
49	47	581	0	38	0	£0.00
50	48	592	0	30	0	£0.00
51	49	616	0	46	0	£0.00
52	50	664	10	76	24	£180.00
53						
54	Total sales	29577		Lost sales	447	
55						

Figure 8.2 The working part of the simulation

produce a number between 0 and 99 (ignoring any figures to the right of the decimal point). For the times when a formula should be as able to return 100 as any other number, a little bit more is needed which is, simply, to add 1 to the total. In this way:

- RAND*11 **equals** A number between 0 and 10.
- (RAND*10)+1 **equals** A number between 1 and 10.
- (RAND*6)+1 **equals** A number between 1 and 6.

How this relates to the simulation is easily explained because the volume of orders being placed on any given day is estimated as between 500 and 750. Therefore, to simulate these sales what is required is a random number somewhere between those limits – a facility which the RAND function offers.

In all cases figures to the right of the decimal point are ignored (assume the INT function has been included in the formula).

To use it, one method would be to simply multiply a random number by the difference between the upper and lower limits. Applying good spreadsheet design rules to this would give a formula something like:

    Random Number*(Highest Figure-Lowest Figure)

The only problem with that is, in the example, it would produce a figure somewhere between 0 and 249 (or 250 if 1 was added to the total). As this is nowhere near the figure required, the trick is to add the base or lowest figure to the number produced to create a formula which in plain English could be described as:

    Random Number*(Highest Figure-Lowest Figure)+Lowest figure

For reasons already explained, 1 would have to be added to this and, also for reasons already explained, the cell references of these figures would have to be made absolute, but otherwise the formula is almost complete. To eliminate any unnecessary decimal fractions, the INT function would have to be included so that the formula in cell M3 becomes:

    =INT(RAND()*($H$14-$H$13)+$H$13+1)

Once this is copied down the column there will be a series of figures which can be thought of as representing the orders received into the system each day.

Other than that there is only one, slightly inconvenient, fact about the RAND function that needs to be known: it recalculates constantly. Every time a figure is entered or changed anywhere in the spreadsheet, a fresh set of random figures will be produced and any other formulas that depend on the results of those figures will be changed accordingly. In some circumstances that might not be a problem, but in others it might be, and it would be confusing in either case. Because of this the recommended procedure when using the RAND function is to set the spreadsheet to manual recalculation. Then no formula will be calculated until the right button is pressed.

- In **Excel** this is done from the Tools menu. Select Options followed by Calculation.

- In **Lotus** this is done from the File menu. Select User Setup, 1-2-3 Preferences, Recalculation.

In both cases select the Manual option and the spreadsheet will not perform any calculations until the F9 key is pressed. This may seem unduly complicated, but once the RAND function is seen in action the benefits will soon become obvious.

Equally obvious is the fact that more work needs to be done on the spreadsheet so, to start with the easiest, the formula in cell P3 is:

```
=IF(M3-$B$6<=0,0,M3-$B$6)
```

Working through this shows that if the sales for a particular day (M3) are less than the capacity of the sales department (B6), there will be no lost sales. On the other hand, if sales are greater than capacity, then the one subtracted from the other gives the number of lost sales. The IF function is needed because there cannot be a negative amount of lost sales and the absolute addressing is needed to keep the formula fixed on the cell for sales capacity when it is copied down the column.

In exactly the same way the cost of those lost sales is the number multiplied by the profit per sale, as shown in cell H15, making the formula for Q3:

```
=P3*$H$15
```

Now things start to get interesting; the potential backlogs need to be calculated.

To start with the admin backlog in cell N3, here several factors which have to be taken into account:

- If admin capacity is greater than sales capacity, the backlog will always be zero.
- If the orders received are greater than the sales capacity, the backlog is sales capacity minus admin capacity.
- If the orders received are smaller than the admin capacity, the backlog will always be zero.
- If none of this is true, the backlog is orders received minus admin capacity.

The reasons for all of this should be obvious after a little thought and are mainly to do with the fact that there cannot be a negative backlog. It also means that the formula for N3 is:

```
=IF(E6>=B6,0,IF(M3>=B6,B6-E6,IF(M3<=E6,0,M3-E6)))
```

If when copying this formula down the column the same figure is constantly repeated, this is not due to an error in the formula. It just means that the new values have yet to be calculated because the spreadsheet has been set to manual recalculation. To produce the correct figures, press F9.

Never be put off by long formulas, or be afraid to create them. In most cases they can be built up slowly and the work can always be spread over several intermediate cells until the logic is proven. It could even be argued that a truly competent spreadsheet user should be able to create formulas longer than this without a second thought. Certainly there will be times when they are needed. As proof, consider the formula in cell N4, which also has to take into account the backlogs from previous days:

```
=IF($E$6>=$B$6,0,IF(M4>=$B$6,($B$6+N3)-$E$6,IF(M4+N3<=$E$6,0,(M4+N3)-
$E$6)))
```

As the absolute cell references signify, this can then be copied down the column.

The assembly backlog

This leaves just the assembly backlog to be calculated. Since this book is about the use of spreadsheets rather than how to create a particular simulation, an overlong explanation of the steps involved in creating this formula would be pointless. Instead, for those who want to try it for themselves, remember that it cannot produce a negative backlog and it must take into account both the number of orders received and the sales capacity, which means that the formula in cell O3 is:

```
=IF(M3<=E6,IF(M3<=H6,0,M3-H6),IF(E6<=H6,0,E6-H6))
```

Similarly, the formula for cell O4, which must take previous backlogs into account, is:

```
=IF(M4+N3<=$E$6,IF(M4+O3<=$H$6,0,M4+O3-$H$6),IF($E$6+N3<=$H$6,
0,$E$6+O3-$H$6))
```

The only point worth making here is the way the IF function has been used. Previously, multiple occurrences of the IF function took the form of the test, the value if true and then the second IF function complete with its arguments. In this case, however, after the first test the value if true was another IF function complete with arguments, while the value if false was a third IF function also with its own arguments. There is nothing too mysterious about it, this just happens to be another way of working which can be useful at times.

There are any number of functions, each with their own way of working. Too many, in fact, for them all to be covered adequately in the help files or reference books, so just because a particular situation is not mentioned does not mean it is impossible. Whenever a solution is required, decide what is needed in plain English, then search for a function that meets at least some, if not all, of the requirements. It is amazing how often a function which at first sight seems to have no valid purpose can suddenly provide the solution.

That said, once the formula is copied down the column all it takes is to enter the total of all sales in cell M54 and the number of lost sales in P54 and the simulation can be completed.

The cost of lost sales in cell E17 is simply the number of lost sales multiplied by the expected profit on orders, which makes the formula:

```
=P54*H15
```

The admin backlog shown in cell E18 is actually the maximum over the period in question and is calculated by the formula:

```
=MAX(N3:N52)
```

With the assembly backlog in E19 being just more of the same, that leaves only the final profit figure in E21 to be calculated. This is the number of orders physically received (total orders minus lost orders) multiplied by the profit per order, from which the total operating costs are subtracted. Here the operating costs are the daily costs shown in B14 multiplied by the number of days over which the simulation is run, as shown in cell L52, to make the formula:

```
=(M54-P54)*H15-(B14*L52)
```

Once this is done and the spreadsheet recalculated as appropriate, it becomes possible to see the simulation in action. Just by changing the number of employees or the process rate, the effect on the operation as a whole can be seen immediately. Not only that, but by looking at the working part of the spreadsheet instead of the display panel, the way the backlogs rise and fall can be seen which, by itself, could be useful when planning staffing levels. In other words, any number of situations can be tried and their effects predicted by computer, which has got to be a lot easier than doing the same thing in real life.

To make things even better, the simulation can also be improved. This introduces another element into the design of spreadsheet simulation which we have deliberately left until now when it was likely to make more sense. This element is to start with only one variable. In the above example it is highly unlikely that every order would attract the same £7.50 profit, but it was fixed at that until the rest of the simulation was working properly (using the sales figures as the only variable). Once that was done the spreadsheet could be changed slightly to show a profit varying randomly between, say, £5 and £10. The best way of doing this would be to use another column in the detail part of the spreadsheet and then enter a formula something like:

```
=RAND()*(10-5)+5+1
```

Once this was copied down the column the number of orders received each day could be multiplied by it to produce the value of orders received. Then the total of that column would become the gross profit before costs were taken into account.

Even in this brief introduction you can see how useful spreadsheet simulation can be. It uses no extra, expensive software, nor is it particularly difficult to do, yet the results can be amazing. The process is both fascinating and rewarding and should be done at every opportunity. The results will more than justify the effort.

Beyond competence

There are some spreadsheet skills which, while by no means difficult to master, are generally thought of as being the sole preserve of the expert. Usually this is because they come dressed up in all manner of strange terminology which scares away the non-expert, yet, like regression analysis, the words used may be technical, but carrying them out is no more difficult than selecting the right choice from the menu.

What follows may be seen as occupying the middle ground between competent and expert, but they are not difficult to understand and since using them can make such a massive difference, they should be learned for that reason alone.

Pivot tables

A pivot table is a way of taking a mass of information which has very little structure to it and rearranging it in a much more meaningful way, both as a form of data analysis and so that further work can be done on the results obtained. Consider the spreadsheet in Figure 9.1.

The first thing to know about pivot tables is that not every spreadsheet can use them. Excel can, but Lotus 123 cannot.

This is the kind of unstructured information mentioned previously. Consider it to be a simple list of orders received, entered as they were received, which could conceivably be found in many organisations. The only snag is that it provides no information for management control purposes. From the list it is impossible to tell which is the top-selling product, what are the total sales per area or who made the most sales. In fact, the information is confused even on a short list such as this. On a much longer list with more products, more areas and a much bigger sales force, that information would be hopelessly lost.

	A	B	C	D
1	Name	Area	Product	Sales
2	Smith	North	AAA	35
3	Jones	South	CCC	35
4	Brown	East	BBB	17
5	Green	West	BBB	16
6	Smith	North	CCC	25
7	Brown	East	AAA	20
8	Smith	North	BBB	15
9	Green	West	CCC	30
10	Jones	South	BBB	18
11	Brown	East	CCC	20
12	Green	West	AAA	30
13	Jones	South	AAA	25
14				

Figure 9.1 A simple list of orders received

What is needed, then, is some way of making sense of all this information without having to create a whole series of different spreadsheets to answer each of the different questions. What is needed, in fact, is a pivot table.

Although these are easy to construct they are a lot harder to explain without an example to refer to and so, the example must come first.

Once the information from Figure 9.1 has been entered into a spreadsheet, select Pivot Table from the data menu. From the dialog box that appears, enter the range A1:D13, which corresponds to the list. Clicking on Next brings up another dialog box and from there select Layout. This will create a display similar to that in Figure 9.2.

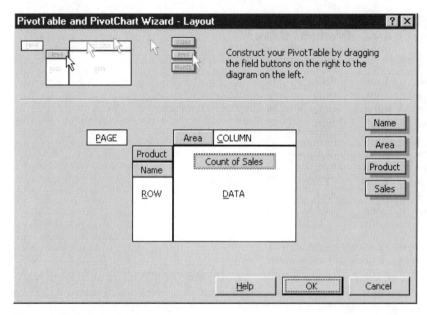

Figure 9.2 A pivot table layout

This has already been completed by dragging the buttons on the right of the diagram on to the pivot table area as shown. Here, for reasons that will be explained later, it is important to do this in the right order. 'Product' must be dragged on to the table before 'Name' so that they appear one beneath the other as they are in the diagram.

Also, when 'Sales' is dragged into the data area, it will change to 'Count of Sales' which is not what is wanted. Count of Sales will show how many orders were listed rather than the total of those orders so, to change that, double-click on the button where it says Count of Sales. This will cause another dialog box to appear. Choose Sum and the display will change to 'Sum of Sales'.

After that, with 'Area' dragged into position, click OK, select where on the spreadsheet the pivot table should appear, and the finished result will look like Figure 9.3.

	E	F	G	H	I	J	K	L
1								
2		Sum of Sales		Area ▾				
3		Product ▾	Name ▾	East	North	South	West	Grand Total
4		AAA	Brown	20				20
5			Green				30	30
6			Jones			25		25
7			Smith		35			35
8		AAA Total		20	35	25	30	110
9		BBB	Brown	17				17
10			Green				16	16
11			Jones			18		18
12			Smith		15			15
13		BBB Total		17	15	18	16	66
14		CCC	Brown	20				20
15			Green				30	30
16			Jones			35		35
17			Smith		25			25
18		CCC Total		20	25	35	30	110
19		Grand Total		57	75	78	76	286
20								

Figure 9.3 A completed pivot table

Now the explanation can begin. Placing 'Product' on the pivot table first meant that the names of the sales force were treated as a sub-category of product sales. The sales of each product were broken down into the name of the person making the sales (which was, in turn, broken down into area). Had 'Name' been placed on the pivot table first then, of course, each individual name would have been treated as the main item, with product a category of that.

From this it becomes possible to work out a few general rules for creating pivot tables.

- **Decide what is to be the focus of the analysis**. (In the example it was product per person and per area, but it could just as easily have been area.) That must be the first item in the row section of the pivot table.

- **Decide what category that main item should be broken down into**. (Names of the sales team in this example.) That must be the second item in the row part of the pivot table.

- **Decide how those categories should be further broken down**. (By area in the example.) That must be shown in the column part of the pivot table.

- **Decide what information is to be summarised**. (Sales in the example.) This fits into the data area of the pivot table.

- **Decide how that information is to be summarised**. (Sum of sales in the example.)

There can be more than just one or two items in the row or columns of a pivot table, although it does start to make things more complicated. Even so, this can be cured by the use of the drop-down menus that appear on all the data labels.

Each one is no more than a list of tick boxes showing all the values listed against that label (Product is a list of all products, Name is a list of all names, and so on). Just deselect or untick any of those boxes and the pivot table will exclude them from all its calculations so that it can concentrate on the items that are left. To see this in action, try it on the pivot table you have just created and it should become apparent why pivot tables are described as an interactive analysis tool.

Arrays

An array is a way of working on more than one cell at the same time. It is also a technique which sounds as if it ought to be difficult when in fact it is incredibly easy. Look at the spreadsheet in Figure 9.4.

	A	B
1	AAA	12
2	BBB	14
3	CCC	15
4	AAA	19
5	BBB	17
6	CCC	13
7		
8		
9	Avg. AAA	15.5

Figure 9.4 Two columns of data

This shows two columns of data and yet using an array formula just an average of those values corresponding to AAA will be calculated. Since the spreadsheet must be told that this is an array formula, it has to be entered by pressing CTRL plus Shift plus Enter simultaneously. The formula to enter is:

```
=AVERAGE(IF(A1:A6="AAA",B1:B6))
```

Any function or any formula can be included, with the sole criterion being that the spreadsheet needs to work on more than one cell (or else why use an array). To see that in practice, try changing the above formula to SUM or MIN or MAX – they will all work just the same. Admittedly it does use a slightly different implementation of the IF function than we have encountered previously, but apart from this there is nothing difficult about using arrays.

Even so, there is slightly more to using them than has been mentioned so far. In the previous example the results of the calculation were shown in one cell, but with arrays it is also possible to have the results appearing in several cells, each one the answer to a different calculation. To demonstrate this, look at the spreadsheet in Figure 9.5.

	E	F	G
1			
2	Col 1	Col 2	Result
3	12	7	94.5
4	13	8	108
5	15	9	121.5
6	14	6	81
7			

Figure 9.5 Working out the average value using a single array formula

This shows a very simple spreadsheet where the average value of Column 1 is multiplied by the individual values of Column 2 to produce the result, using a single array formula.

The first thing to know about entering array formulas which produce results over more than one cell is that first of all the relevant cells must be highlighted. In this case that would mean highlighting G3:G6 and then, remembering to enter it with CTRL+Shift+Enter, the formula is:

    =AVERAGE($E$3:$E$6)*F3:F6

The absolute references are there to make sure the right cell range is calculated. Any time a formula is in danger of becoming too complex, or of needing the results from too many other cells, an array calculation will very likely solve the problem. For that reason alone the technique should be learned. It is too valuable to ignore.

Macros

At their most basic, macros are a way of automating repetitive tasks, using one key stroke to replace several. That may seem like a job best left to the experts, but in reality nothing could be easier. The only slight problem is, explaining how to do it risks becoming long and complicated, which means the easiest way of doing it is by example.

In Figure 9.6 the only calculation involved is profit which is, of course, sales multiplied by selling price (S.P.). To set the level of those sales use the version or scenario manager so that one version is 10,000 and name it 'Best' while another, to be named 'Worst', is 5,000. (Also ignore the title at the top of the spreadsheet, as that will be dealt with later.)

If there has been one central theme running throughout this book it is that what appears difficult is usually very simple. Macros are no exception. They might be the first step towards programming, but that just makes them useful, not difficult.

	A	B	C	D
1				
2			BEST CASE	
3				
4		Sales	S. P.	Profit
5		10000	£15.00	£150,000.00
6				

Figure 9.6 A best case spreadsheet

When you have done this, it will be a perfect example of a repetitive task that could be automated. Instead of going through all the key presses, or mouse clicks, necessary to display a different version, a macro could be called up to do this automatically. Not only will this save time and effort, it also means anyone can use the spreadsheet to its fullest extent without even having to know what a version manager is, or how to display one.

With macros being so useful, learning how to create them will always be a good idea – especially as it involves nothing more than choosing the right menu option.

All spreadsheets have the facility to record whatever keys are pressed, or menu options chosen. When such a recording is played back this is known as a macro.

First of all the recorder has to be activated, which in Excel is done from the Tools menu followed by Macro, Record New Macro, and in Lotus from the Edit menu followed by Scripts and Macros, Record script. In both cases a dialog box will appear asking for the macro to be given a name. To keep things simple, call this macro 'Best' and then:

- in cell C2 enter BEST CASE;

- go through whatever menu options are needed to display the scenario or version 'Best'.

At this point stop the recorder from running, either by following the menu options (Stop Recording is right next to Record New Macro) or by using the display panel which will have appeared on the screen. This will have controls which look and act like those on a cassette recorder, so press the Stop button.

Repeat the entire process, except in C2 enter WORST CASE, name the macro 'Worst' and display the version also known as Worst. There will then be two macros which change the version automatically and even put a title across the spreadsheet to say which is which. Now practice using them.

Running a macro

There is more than one way to run a macro. The first is from the menu system – select the Run Macro option (next to the Record Macro option) and choose the name of the macro to be run. While this works, it is long-winded because effectively it just replaces one set of key strokes for another.

An alternative is to use what is sometimes referred to as a hot key combination. This means a combination of two keys are assigned to a particular macro so that when these are pressed simultaneously the macro runs automatically. By convention one of these keys will be CTRL and when the macro is first named the same dialog box also includes an option to choose the second key. In this way, for example, CTRL+B could be the combination which activates the best macro, with CTRL+W activating the worst.

For Lotus users the system is to press Alt + F3. This displays a list of all macros from which the right one can be chosen.

While this method is much easier to use, it does have one disadvantage – you have to either remember the various key combinations, which is not always easy, or there must be written instructions somewhere on the spreadsheet telling the user which keys activate which macros. Quite apart from the fact that this can look ugly, or even confusing, on a spreadsheet with many of the cells already being used, there might not be room for these notes. They could be put somewhere else, but having to scroll across three screens' worth of spreadsheet just to find a note listing the macro key combinations will never be user-friendly – and that pre-supposes the user knows the notes are there in the first place.

What is needed is a method which is easy to use and requires no special instructions. Something like a button which could be included in the spreadsheet and which could then run the macro at the click of a mouse. That may sound fantastic, but in fact it can be done extremely easily.

All spreadsheets have what is known as a script editor built into them. This is a method of collating all macros and any other pieces of programming into one unit so the one can be used to run the other. One specialised piece of programming will put a button on the screen and the script editor will connect that to a macro, so pressing the button will make the macro work. First, however, no matter which spreadsheet you are using, the script editor will look something like that in Figure 9.7.

Script editor in Excel
First of all you need the Control Toolbox. This can be found by right-clicking on the menu bar at the top of the screen. A list of options (also known as toolbars) will appear, of which one will be Control Toolbox.

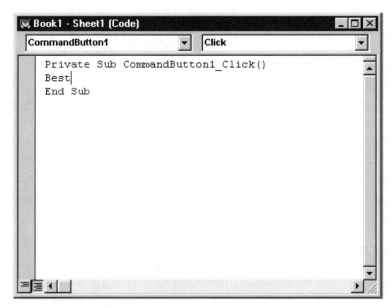

Figure 9.7 The script editor

Look for the icon with a set square on it and click on this to enter Design Mode. Then click on Command Button. At this point the spreadsheet cursor will change into cross-hairs which can be used to position the button anywhere on the spreadsheet.

Once that is done and the button appears, right-click on it and from the menu choose CommandButton Object followed by Edit. At this point a word processor-style cursor will appear over the button which will currently read: CommandButton 1. Delete this and type in 'BEST'. Then, to finish the editing, click anywhere else on the spreadsheet.

Once again right-click over the button and this time choose View Code. This brings up the script editor into which the name of the macro ('Best') should be entered exactly as it appears in Figure 9.7.

Exit from the script editor, click on the design (set square) icon to exit Design Mode, and the job is done.

Now repeat the process, only this time label the button 'WORST' and in the script editor enter the name of the worst macro.

Script editor in Lotus

On the toolbar at the top of the screen there is a button icon. Click on that and the spreadsheet cursor will change into cross-hairs which can be used to position the button anywhere on the spreadsheet. The script editor will automatically appear and the name of the macro ('Best') should be entered into it exactly as shown in Figure 9.7. After that exit from the script editor.

Now right-click on the button and from the menu options choose Drawing Properties. A dialog box will appear and in the area marked Text enter 'BEST'. Exit from this and the job is done.

Now repeat the process, except in the script editor enter the name of the worst macro and under Drawing Properties enter 'WORST'.

In both cases there will be two buttons on the spreadsheet, one marked 'BEST' and the other 'WORST'. Simply clicking on a particular button will activate whichever macro is associated with it and, in this case, the version will be displayed. Clicking the other button will change to the other version automatically.

Conclusion

As this book has shown, spreadsheets are neither difficult to use, nor do they call for any advanced amount of computer literacy. All it really takes to use one is the confidence to put together a few functions so that they make a formula, or to select an option from the menu, along with the knowledge of how to use them.

You will gain this knowledge from this book, from the help files, from any other books and, just as importantly, from studying other spreadsheets. By finding out how they work and how their formulas were implemented, you can learn some valuable lessons. You can then put these lessons to good use when you need to build other spreadsheets.

As for the confidence, that will come mainly from practice and experience, but you should have gained a fair measure of these already just by working through the examples in this book. Once you have learned these basic techniques you can build on them and use spreadsheet programs for what they really are: the most powerful and flexible business analysis tool yet devised.

Use your spreadsheet program to its full extent and enjoy the benefits it will bring.

Index